RUN,
RINSE,
REPEAT

Dana,

Wishing you much
health + happiness — Enjoy!

Coach
Bob

RUN, RINSE, REPEAT

THE STORY OF A COACH, A TEAM AND A PASSION FOR RUNNING

Mike Boza

authorHOUSE®

AuthorHouse™
1663 Liberty Drive
Bloomington, IN 47403
www.authorhouse.com
Phone: 1-800-839-8640

Published by AuthorHouse   09/12/2012

ISBN: 978-1-4772-6437-9 (sc)
ISBN: 978-1-4772-6436-2 (e)

Library of Congress Control Number: 2012915829

For Linda . . . The best part of me is you.

CONTENTS

FALLING IN LOVE AGAIN

"When are you going to write your book?"

My friend and mentor Dr. Dennis Jones caught me off guard with this question shortly after we hopped into our golf cart and headed down the cart path to find our opening tee shots. As much as I respect and trust my good friend's counsel, the idea of me writing a book seemed to come out of left field. I have been a teacher and a coach for thirty years, and I had never considered the possibility of writing a book.

"What could I write about?" I asked.

"All of it," Dennis replied. "You're a hall of fame coach with five state championships and you were Plant High School's teacher of the year. You grew up in a difficult situation and yet you still managed make a beautiful family of your own and raise two great kids. It's time to think about the lessons you've learned that got you this far and start passing them along."

Dennis's inflated perception of my importance is skewed by the role I played in his son Victor's life as his teacher and cross country coach. What I do is not much different than what thousands of teachers and coaches around the country do every day. But when someone makes a positive difference in your son or daughter's life, you never forget it. I figured this was just another way for Dennis to tell me what I meant in his son's life.

Every man and woman needs a guide like Dennis to help them work through the challenges of life and strive to reach their fullest potential. Before he retired, Dennis traveled around the world as an organizational psychologist, consulting for businesses to make them more successful. Now, he devotes his talents, time and energy to doing the same for his family, his friends and his community. And here he is on the first fairway encouraging me to consider writing a book.

The discussion regarding my future as a writer didn't last long as we eventually made it to our tee shots and turned our attention to club selection for the second shot on the long, narrow par five.

It was flattering to think that someone with Dennis's credentials considered my life to be worth learning from, and the thought of writing a book definitely resonated in my mind for a while longer. Maybe I do have something to write that's worth reading.

It makes me uncomfortable to talk about the awards and championships I have won because I don't like to brag or sound arrogant. But if I'm trying to decide if I have what it takes to write a book, I suppose I owe it to myself to briefly browse through my trophy case. I have been a successful teacher and coach for many years, but I don't often think of myself that way. Like most people, I tend to compare myself to those ahead of me. Most of us are never really satisfied with what we obtain because we tend to compare ourselves to those who have more than we do.

For me, it's not about material things. As my wife Linda said recently, "We have what we want, and we want what we have." Neither of us spends much time thinking about having better clothes, nicer cars or even a bigger home. But I do have a very strong achievement motivation that constantly drives me to be the best at whatever I do. It's been that drive as much as anything else which has contributed to my successes—and to my failures. I've never been too afraid to set high goals.

As long as there are teams with more titles and teachers with higher pass rates, I will be looking for ways to improve. One of those ways has been reading books. Ever since I started running regularly, I've been reading about running. I'm pretty sure that I've read more about running and training in the past 25 years than I read about any single subject during my formal education. If there is anything I do feel qualified to write about, it's running and coaching.

The next time that the thought of writing a book crossed my mind was a few months later while I was reading Haruki Murakami's *What I Talk About When I Talk About Running*. In this memoir, the author tells the story of his preparation for the 2005 New York City Marathon while reflecting on his life's journey. Reading the book helped me rediscover something that I had been missing for some time—my passion for running.

As my passion for running was being reignited, I started to have one of those falling-in-love experiences, when your thoughts become consumed by the object of your affection. We sometimes do crazy things when we are "falling in love" with someone or something. In this case, I came up with the crazy idea to do something similar to what Murakami did. I decided to run the ING Miami Marathon in January of 2012 (my first in over five years) and write a book about the journey as the months progressed.

So I started this memoir on April 29, 2011. I wanted to write the kind of book that I would enjoy reading. Anytime I go into a bookstore, I search the sports and fitness sections for books written by runners or coaches that share useful insights on training or tell stories of great runners and epic races.

In 1998, runner and author Chris Lear followed the University of Colorado Buffaloes throughout their cross country season. His book, *Running with the Buffaloes,* features an in-depth look into the storied program as well as its legendary coach, Mark Whetmore, who has his own unique style and high intensity training philosophy. The book was a huge hit with high school and college runners and coaches, and it remains popular with that crowd mainly because there are so few books about cross country out there.

Another favorite book of mine is *God on the Starting Line: The Triumph of a Catholic School Running Team and Its Jewish Coach*, by Marc Bloom. I liked this book even better because I could relate to the author since it was a story of a high school team. The stories in his book reminded me of what I go through every day with my own team. Some of them are insightful and some are hilarious. I want to include those kinds of stories into my book.

During the months leading up to my marathon, I will be training a group of 35 boys as they attempt to win the first boys cross country championship in our school's long history. Over the past few years, I have made numerous presentations to groups of coaches interested in knowing the "secrets" of successful cross country coaching. Hopefully, the stories that follow will document the dramatic details of an historic season in progress.

Right now, my thoughts are consumed by the possibilities that lie ahead of me in the next few months, but I am also worried. I haven't really tested myself as a runner in about five years, and last year I suffered my first major running injury. I had surgery in May of 2010 to repair a torn meniscus in my right knee. I have no real idea of just how much fitness I have lost or how long it's going to take regain it. I do have nearly nine months to prepare for the ING Miami Marathon, and I have plenty of experience training for and completing over a dozen marathons. But I still feel like I am recovering from the surgery, and part of me is wondering if my body can hold up to the strain of all the miles I will need to run to prepare successfully for the 26.2-mile challenge. What if I get injured again? I suppose the fact that this challenge scares me is largely what makes it so irresistible and worthwhile.

When I first began setting running goals over two decades ago, I would create a plan for several months of training and literally check off each workout day by day. That always motivated me because I hated to see empty spaces instead of checks. I learned over time that sometimes I got so focused on checking all those boxes that I lost focus on what I was really trying to accomplish. Eventually, I learned to do without those master plans and just feel my way through training programs. This time, my motivation is going to be writing the story. Every run, every turn and every up and down for myself and my team will be something to write about. I'm anxious to get started and even more anxious to know how it will end.

Though there will be tips that some runners and coaches might find useful or interesting, this is not a book about how to train for a marathon or coach a cross country team. As I tell the stories of my training for the ING Miami Marathon and my team's quest for an historic state championship, I will reflect on my journey as a runner and a coach and the lessons I have learned from winning and losing along the way. Mostly though, I hope to share my passion for running, a sport that I know has made me happier, healthier and even smarter.

Chapter One
WILD BILL

This book is about running as much as anything else. My life is certainly more than running, but it is clearly one of the things that helps define me. Though I have coached numerous state champion runners and teams over the years, I'm not a great runner by any means. I didn't run competitively in high school or college, and I've never even been close to winning a road race of any distance. But for the latter half of my 51-year life, I've spent as much time and energy running and studying running as I have on anything besides my family and my career as a teacher. I truly love running.

Psychologist M. Scott Peck defines love as "the will to extend one's self for the purpose of nurturing one's own or another's spiritual growth." In his book, *The Road Less Traveled*, Peck distinguishes "romantic love" (falling in love) from "real love" by pointing out that "falling" into anything requires no work at all. "Real love," he argued, requires some work. I agree. In fact, sometimes the work we do to really love someone (or something—like running) can be pretty darn hard.

Most people can't possibly appreciate the hard work that my wife Linda and I have put into our happy marriage. Ours is the envy of many who dreamed about finding the elusive fairy-tale, happily-ever-after romance. We met at 17 and married at 19 while we were still in college. We've raised two great kids and supported each other in good times and bad, just like we promised to do over 31 years ago.

As far as anyone can tell from the outside, marriage has been as easy for us as falling in love. But regardless of how easy we make it look, we didn't just stumble into a fairy tale. Like most things in life that are really worthwhile, it's taken discipline, patience, self-sacrifice and plenty of old-fashioned hard work. For me, it's also meant struggling to break some deep-rooted habits learned (or maybe inherited?) from parents who were unable to love each other effectively.

1

Most people have the opposite perception of my love relationship with running.

"How can you possibly enjoy running all those miles?" I regularly get asked similar questions from people when they find out how much I run. From the outside, I'm sure it looks like torture to some people. Most non-runners have only painful memories of their own limited experiences related to running. After all, many sports use running as punishment for everything from being late to goofing off at practice.

Few people can appreciate how much I get out of running or how effortless it can sometimes feel. As I will discuss later on in this book, I believe that running has not only made me healthier, but happier and smarter too. In fact, considering the many ways in which running has made me better, it's just as fair to say that running loves me, too.

That might freak some folks out.

I first fell in love with running over 25 years ago. Like any long-term relationship, we've had our ups and downs. For the past four or five years, we have mainly just co-existed. When we were really hot and heavy, I was running several races a year. I became obsessed with qualifying for the Boston Marathon and, after over a decade of failures, I finally reached that standard for my age group in 2000 with a time that is still my personal best for the marathon—3 hours and 17 minutes.

But since my second Boston Marathon in 2006, I have had no real interest in racing. Since I haven't been racing, I haven't felt the need to train very hard or with much focus. It was ironic, then, that it was during this period of relatively low-level running (for me) that I suffered my first real injury.

Sometimes love hurts, I suppose.

In preparation for the ING Miami Marathon, I've started to record my running mileage every day in a running journal. My plan is to slowly build up my monthly mileage from about 100 miles in May 2011 to about 200 miles for the months of December 2011 and January 2012. I ran four times over the final six days of April for a total of 25 miles. This is the type of weekly mileage I will need to maintain during May to reach 100 miles for the month. My legs are sore from the sudden increase in the mileage and frequency of my running, but I've had no pain in my knee.

Most of my running will be done on Tampa's beautiful Bayshore Boulevard. It's a short one-mile trip from my house. The 8-foot wide, 4.5-mile long sidewalk can often get crowded, but there is also a grassy path that varies in width and pretty much runs parallel for the entire distance. Although the Bayshore can reek of decaying sea creatures during low tides, the views of Tampa's waterfront and skyline are spectacular.

Our Plant High School distance runners also do most of their training on the Bayshore because it is so conveniently located in our district. Only one of our runners qualified for next Saturday's state meet, so this spring's track season is technically over for the rest of the guys. I like to keep all of the varsity runners training together through the state meet, so the remainder of the boys will compete in a couple of local 5K races over the next two weeks. After those races, the boys will have about four weeks off from structured training before we start to practice regularly again.

Most of our boys train with me year-round with only two 4-week breaks in the calendar year—one in December and one in May. Believe it or not, many of our runners are so motivated to succeed, they have to be practically forced to take a few days off from running. Kids today . . . right? Contrary to what too many folks my age seem to think, today's kids have more pressure on them than ever before.

I grew up in between two distinct paradigms regarding childhood play. In my parents' generation, kids mostly "played." Ad hoc games in the neighborhood were more common than formal, competitive sports leagues. By the time I began to raise my own two children, the pressure for young kids to commit to an organized sports program was strong. Children who are not playing in a competitive baseball or soccer league during their elementary school years, for example, sometimes risk being left too far behind to compete in high school.

Many children today and their parents feel pressure to get kids involved in formal sports training as soon as possible. There is also great pressure for kids to specialize as soon as possible in one sport. It's a rare student-athlete these days who can play several different sports successfully. It's not just because of the physical constraints, but often the pressure placed on them by demanding coaches (like myself) to play one sport year-round in order to maximize the benefits of their sport.

My daughter Melody started a formal dance program at the age of 3, and so did most of her classmates at the performing arts high school she attended. By the time she entered middle school, her days consisted of a tightly packed schedule of school, practice, meals and homework. Without this daily regimen, she would likely never have qualified for acceptance to that performing arts high school or won the scholarship that helped her continue her passion in college.

Melody was never pressured by Linda or me to push as hard as she did to become a successful dancer. In fact, both of us did our best to help her keep her life balanced by encouraging her to try other things. I tried introducing her to everything from running (of course) to tennis and even golf. I tried teaching her how to throw and catch just about every kind of ball, but all to no avail.

At one point, when Melody was in sixth grade, she briefly re-considered the extent of her commitment to dance. She casually mentioned the possibility of being more of a well-rounded kid and maybe even playing a sport like basketball. When my wife mentioned this to the middle school basketball coach at Melody's school, Linda was dismayed by the coach's response.

"Oh please, not another kid who doesn't know how to play!" she said. It was a sad testimony on the difficulty that some kids face today when they try to be better-rounded.

My son Andrew was quite a different story. As a little boy, Andrew was usually quite content just to play the way his grandparents might have done. Most of the time, his childhood play time amounted to making up scenarios with other kids in the neighborhood in which they imagined themselves to be on some sort of adventure. Sometimes they would get involved in a makeshift game of football or basketball, but that was never Andrew's preference.

I began "gently guiding" him into organized sports when he was about 6. Maybe I was like some of those parents today who push their kids into organized sports so they don't get left out later on. Maybe my macho ego wanted to be vicariously fed by watching my son excel on the athletic field. At the time, I would have claimed that I merely wanted him to reap the benefits of organized sports. During his elementary school years, he tried tee ball, kung-fu, soccer camp, basketball leagues and even pee wee football.

Andrew has natural speed and coordination, so he was always fairly competent at everything he tried. He's also very intelligent and coachable, which usually made him an asset to whatever team he played on. All he lacked was the passion for sport that drives a player to stand out. None of these sports ever really grabbed him. Whenever a season would end, he rarely gave it a second thought until I brought it up again.

By the time he was in middle school, he started finding success as a runner. His middle school offered both cross country and track, and it was here that Andrew's intelligence, maturity and natural self-discipline helped him stand out above his peers in a way he had not been able to do in his other athletic endeavors. Of course, this pleased me immensely.

The fact that he was obviously good at the sport was enough to motivate him to commit to it in a way he had not done with any previous sport. Even before Andrew was old enough to join the Jesuit High School team that I was coaching at the time, he was training with my team during the summer and he even attended our summer team camp in North Carolina. This extra training was definitely more my idea than his, and I regularly second-guessed myself regarding the way I was bringing him into the sport. Though I never saw any signs that he was unhappy about it, I also never saw any signs that he was developing a real passion for running. If he had resisted, or if he had shown a passionate interest in some other pursuit, I think (I hope) I would have backed off.

Andrew went on to have a very successful high school running career. He was talented, dedicated and fearless. Before he graduated from Jesuit, we won our school's first state championship in track and another (our 3rd) in cross country. He never grew to love running in the way that I have, but even in high school Andrew was wise enough to see the good that it was bringing him. He had good friends on the team, he was recognized around school as part of something special and, of course, it helped bring the two of us very close together.

One day when Andrew was just a sophomore in high school, he casually announced to Linda and me that he wanted to attend the U.S. Naval Academy for college. This took both of us by surprise. We were quite shocked, very proud and more than a little bit nervous. We were nervous primarily because it would mean putting himself in harm's way. But we were also nervous because, as educators, we both understood the difficulty of getting accepted into Annapolis.

He later decided to pursue the U.S. Military Academy at West Point instead, but the main idea was still the same. How was our son going to distinguish himself from the thousands of others competing for those limited spots? Even though he was an excellent student and an all-around great kid, his application would have been incomplete without having demonstrated his discipline and commitment as captain of a state-champion cross country team.

There is no doubt that running helped Andrew get into West Point, and being a member of the West Point cross country and track teams his first year definitely helped him cope with the unique rigors of life as a West Point plebe (West Point's term for freshmen). But when he reached the college level of running and the expectations got even more stressful, it was no longer bringing him the same success and satisfaction he enjoyed in high school.

In the precious few moments of free time he had during his high school years, Andrew discovered the sport that became his true passion—paintball. After enduring a year of college running that was hindered by stress injuries, Andrew decided to give up cross country and track to join West Point's emerging paintball squad. As soon as he did, we all realized that this was the kind of play he'd always been looking for. The fire was lit. Before he left West Point, Andrew helped forge this relatively new team into a competitive intercollegiate squad that travelled around the country competing in national events.

In contrast to Melody and Andrew's childhood "play" experiences, mine was far more spontaneous. Whereas Melody was following a busy dance schedule and Andrew was being formed into a runner, I just seemed to randomly wander into things.

My earliest running memory was when I was about 10 years old. My uncle Mandy was visiting from North Dakota where he was stationed with the Air Force. He was short, dark-skinned, and very fit. He had a hairy chest and arms, and he wore his hair in a military-style flat-top. Uncle Mandy was full of positive energy and he exuded the classic 1950s can-do military personality. He decided one morning that I was going to accompany him for a jog during his visit, so I put on my tennis shoes and innocently followed him out the door.

We jogged one mile to a bridge near my house, turned around and headed back. He talked the entire way, and he acted very proud of me when we were finished. Uncle Mandy returned home to North Dakota, and it was years before I ever went jogging again, but a seed was definitely planted that day. Though my first run was an uncomfortable struggle for most of the 20 minutes or so, the glow of my achievement lasted for some time. It was my first encounter with the real joy of running—a joy that transcends the minutes and hours spent grinding along.

Perhaps the most fortuitous "wandering" I ever did was into the The Great Malenko's health studio when I was only about 13 years old. "Boris Malenko" was born Lawrence J. Simon in New Jersey in 1933. He was a professional wrestler who became a popular villain in the early days of the sport by claiming to be from Moscow, Russia, during the height of the Cold War. He was fairly small (about 5'9") compared to most professional wrestlers, but to me he was larger than life.

His son Shelly played with me on a Police Athletic League (PAL) football team and lived nearby. One summer day, we were just hanging out together roaming the neighborhood, and we wandered into his father's health studio, located less than half a mile from my house. I was blown away. I had no idea that Shelly's dad was The Great Malenko. In those days he was in the latter stages of his wrestling career and was best known to me for a locally famous television commercial in which he "wrestled" a mattress from a local bedding firm.

"Not even The Great Malenko can destroy our mattresses," the announcer would say.

Except for his classic wrestler's physique and his trademark mustache, nothing else about him was like the character I saw on television. I remember him as a kind, thoughtful man—the opposite of the nasty Cold War Russian villain he played in the ring. And he didn't speak with the same, thick Russian accent I heard him use on TV. Shelly and I made more visits to his dad's gym in the days to come, and eventually Mr. Simon invited me to train with his son and the others (many were professional wrestlers) in his studio. He also encouraged Shelly and me to do some easy jogging a couple days a week as part of our regimen.

Mr. Simon took time to show me his unique training methods. The workouts focused mainly on strength, but also put a strong emphasis on flexibility and agility. There was a universal weight machine in the middle of the room and some other standard weight equipment around the perimeter, but what made his training truly unique (and fun) was the use of makeshift equipment, like weighted bowling pins, that required you to combine strength and coordination at the same time. By the end of that summer I could go into a back bridge from a standing position and do several reps of handstand push-ups with my feet resting on the wall.

Prior to that summer, I never had much self-confidence as an athlete. I was a chubby little kid for most of my childhood. I played little league baseball for a couple of years, but I was certainly no stand out. I had moderate success in PAL football (where I met Shelly), but that was mostly based on my "enthusiastic" approach. What I lacked in speed, agility and overall talent, I tried to make up for with effort and hustle. Football coaches seemed to appreciate that more than baseball coaches.

Malenko's (er, I mean Mr. Simon's) training program could not have come at a better time in my life. I was a regular customer (though I don't remember ever having to pay) during the summer before I entered high school. That was the year that my body underwent the pivotal transformation from a boy's to a man's. In fact, I've only gained one inch of height since my freshman year of high school. Between the rush of hormones and the steady training I was getting, it was as if I was born again by the time I showed up for football tryouts prior to my freshman year of high school.

I soon emerged as a pretty good outside linebacker, and I was one of only four freshmen invited to join the varsity team my sophomore year. Along with the physical changes came the inevitable psychological and emotional transformation. My new physical stature started to give me a sense of confidence and efficacy that I never had in elementary or middle school. The fact that I went to an all-male, Catholic school that placed great value on being "macho," definitely exaggerated my sense of worth. You might even say all of my newfound physical prowess made me pretty obnoxious.

Not only was I one of the few sophomores to play varsity football at Jesuit High School in 1975, but that year also turned out to be one of the best seasons in our school's storied history which included a state championship in 1968. Three weeks into what would be our school's first undefeated season, our starting outside linebacker injured himself in a skateboarding accident. Though I was technically third-string, I sensed that I had been outplaying the second-string linebacker in practice, and I thought I had a really good chance to make the starting lineup for the next Friday night game.

After school that Monday, all I could think about was getting to practice to earn that starting position. Before I reached the athletic fields, my geometry teacher, Martha Connors, stopped me.

"Do you realize that you still owe me three homework assignments?" she asked. Ms. Connors was my favorite teacher. She was a big sports fan, very proud of her Irish heritage and a HUGE Notre Dame fan. I actually liked geometry. It was the first math course that I felt confident in, and Ms. Connors was the main reason. She was a great teacher, and she really made me feel good about myself academically in a way that I rarely did in other classes.

"No problem, Ms. Connors, I promise I'll get all caught up by the end of the week," I replied smiling. I was anxious to get out on the field and earn my spot in the starting lineup of this historic team.

"No, Mr. Boza, you'll be making those up today," she said confidently.

My heart sunk. "You don't understand, Ms. Connors, I NEED to get to practice today. I might be in the starting lineup this week."

"I already talked to Coach Minahan about this, and he says it's okay. He said he doesn't really need you until you're done with your geometry homework."

I was confused, frustrated and furious. Since it was a Monday, I missed our weekly "skull session," where the coaches would break down the previous week's performances and provide us with scouting reports on our next opponent. By the time I got my homework done, the team was wrapping up the main portion of practice and preparing for conditioning drills. To make it worse, I had to stay after conditioning drills and do more punishment running for missing practice—no wonder so many people learn to hate running.

I've never stopped thanking Martha Connors for doing that to me. It changed my life as a student. I rarely missed any more homework assignments (I NEVER missed any more geometry assignments), and my grades improved dramatically in all of my classes from that point on. Martha later went on to marry my football coach. I suppose that's why she could tell him who was coming to practice and who wasn't.

Where The Great Malenko left off, Coach "Wild Bill" Minahan picked up. No coach or teacher has had a greater effect on me than this former marine, Korean War veteran and University of Tampa football legend. His fiery, passionate style and his old-school methods of discipline earned him the nickname "Wild Bill." Many of the things he did and said to us back then could get a coach fired today, but it was exactly what I needed and even wanted.

I loved Wild Bill. We all did—even when we hated him. He was hard, but he was consistent and fair. When you screwed up, he let you have it. But when you came through, he spared no energy or words showing his approval. This is what I got from Wild Bill—excitement, passion, and unbridled enthusiasm!

According to Wild Bill, "If you're gonna do something, do it with some goddam energy and enthusiasm or don't do it at all!"

By the time I was a senior, I walked around Jesuit High School like I owned the place. Somehow, using our roles as student council executives, my friend Rudy Fernandez and I even managed to have our own office space in a small room behind the chapel. I'm sure there were more than a few kids at school that hated my guts for being such a cocky loudmouth. Those kids' dream came true when I got my nose bloodied and quickly lost a boxing match that the student council put on in the gym after school one day to raise money for overseas Jesuit missions.

"You're a lover, not a fighter," Coach Minahan said to me after my humiliating boxing debut.

I needed that uppercut to the nose. I needed everything Jesuit gave me. Jesuit became my home even more than my own family, which was disintegrating steadily around me. My parents were each battling their own demons, not the least of which was the fact that their marriage was all but over. Because they were both so distracted, I was left with plenty of independence. Luckily for me, my teachers, coaches and teammates were always there to give my life stability and purpose. There's no doubt in my mind that my calling to teach and coach was born in that time and place.

I've spent most of my career trying to do for other young men what
Wild Bill did for me.
(Photo courtesy of Bill and Martha Minahan)

Chapter Two
THE MACHO MARATHON

My first couple weeks of training for the 2012 ING Miami Marathon are behind me now, and, except for feeling the chronic fatigue normally associated with an increase in training, things are going very well. I'm still on pace to run 100 miles by the end of May. I've been careful to keep my pace very easy throughout the majority of my runs. Yesterday was a Sunday, and I did an eight-mile run on the hilly, residential roads of Temple Terrace where I did the majority of my long runs years ago during the peak of my marathon training. This neighborhood has long been popular with runners because of its wide, quiet streets and ample shade on the tree-lined riverfront route. As much as I prefer trail running over roads, the Temple Terrace road course is much more similar to the type of running one does in a marathon.

Running these roads along the Hillsborough River reminds me of my childhood neighborhood a couple of miles downstream. During my high school years, I periodically jogged along the river when I was getting ready for football season to start. The last thing you want to do is show up to the first day of two-a-day workouts without being in decent shape. There were always some idiots who showed up to those hot, summer workouts only to puke their guts out.

"You spent your summer putting poisons in your body and lying around the house, didn't you, you goddam piss-ant?" Wild Bill would shout at those unfortunates without an ounce of sympathy. I never wanted that to be me Wild Bill was yelling at.

When I decided to try to play football in college, I found out running was a requirement to make the team. The literature that the Furman University coaches sent to prospective walk-ons described in detail the workouts we should be doing prior to arriving at camp. These workouts included two very specific running requirements: a 6-minute mile and a 60-second quarter mile. I remember going to my high school track and trying both of these challenges one summer afternoon. The results were very discouraging.

When I arrived in the foothills of South Carolina to try out for the Furman University football team, the first physical tests we took were in the weight room. I wasn't very big or strong (especially compared to today's incoming college freshman), but I remember surprising myself with how well I did. The summer before leaving Tampa, I worked hard to finally bench press over 200 lbs. During my max-out test at Furman, with all of these strange guys around cheering me on, I was able to bench 225 lbs. I laugh when I think about that now because many of the high school football kids that I currently teach in my A.P. psychology classes can bench that weight several times in a row.

Then, it was out to the track. We started with the 6-minute mile test. Again, I was surprised at how much easier it was when I was 600 miles from home, running for my life (or so it seemed) with all these strange, new people around me. I finished with 10 seconds to spare in about 5:50. There were a few players who didn't make it, and I was feeling pretty good about myself until I realized that a couple of the older guys were laughing at me for the way I was grunting and pounding my fist to my chest in the final lap to psyche myself through it. It was not a smooth first impression. Then it got worse.

The coaches decided to cancel the 40-yard dash. That was actually good for me because, like I usually tell people who can't believe I played college football, "Hey, I was small, but I was slow." We moved instead to the final event of the day, the 440-yard run. To stay on the team, we needed to run it under 60 seconds. Again, as I write this today, I am embarrassed. Most of my varsity runners can do this without much problem. I was nervous about it because, in my rehearsal for this back in Tampa, I barely broke 65 seconds—and it really hurt. But after my success with the bench press and the mile run, I figured that I would definitely run much faster. I did. I finished in 61 seconds.

It turns out that those Furman football coaches took their fitness standards for walk-ons seriously. They took me and a few other guys who didn't make it over to the side and told us that we were to report to the track at 6 a.m. the next morning to try again. If we didn't make it, we'd get up at 6 a.m. every morning and do it over and over until we met the standard. The next morning, my roommate Tommy (who also missed the 60-second standard) and I walked in the darkness across the dew-covered field in front of our dorm over to the track where a coach was waiting for us. He called the four of us over and made us do a few stretches. After a few minutes, he lined us up on the start and yelled "go."

I was still stiff and sore from the previous day's effort. The four of us gave all we had for one big lap in the darkness, but none of us made it. In fact, my time was even slower this time.

"See you boys tomorrow morning," the coach uttered as he walked away from us in apparent disgust. To make it worse, we could see the rest of the team starting to arrive for our 6:30 a.m. practice which consisted mainly of strenuous conditioning drills. Not exactly what I needed or wanted at that point.

At 3:30 p.m., we were back on the field for the second practice of the day. This time there were skill drills and some learning sessions that weren't as physically strenuous, but practice finished with 30 minutes of various kinds of running. The last 10 minutes we spent running "banks," which were basically 30-yard sprints up a steep bank on the field in front of my dorm.

At dinner that night, I was almost too tired to eat. Tommy, who was a quiet kid from some small town in South Carolina, was on his second plate of food before I was halfway done with mine. Tommy was smaller than me and obviously not much faster. Sadly, I took consolation in this. I was glad not to be alone in this struggle. We looked like an odd pair. I stood out on the team as one of the very few Hispanic players. I had my dark hair cut very short, and my skin was bronzed from the Florida summer. Tommy was more typical of the other white players. He was fair-skinned with stringy blond hair that reached his shirt collar. I finally got up the nerve to ask him the question that was on my mind all day.

"Have you thought about quitting?" I asked.

He paused briefly and looked up from his food. "They can try to run me off all they want, but they ain't gonna make me quit."

"Me neither," I said. I spent all evening trying to convince myself I could wake up before dawn the next day and run a quarter mile under 60 seconds. By the time I fell asleep, I think I had myself nearly convinced I could do it. But that confidence was a distant dream by the time I woke up and started to drag myself across the field back to the track. Somehow, it felt even darker, warmer and stickier outside than it had the previous morning. The coach was even less enthusiastic than the previous day, and the other two guys never showed up. I never saw either of them again.

Tommy and I pushed each other as hard as we could. We were side-by-side when the coach hollered out, "Sixty!" Unfortunately, there were still about 15 to 20 yards of straightaway left before the finish line. He didn't even call out our final time, though we did manage to get closer than the day before. The coach walked away and left us there without mentioning whether or not we should come back the next morning. I wanted to quit, but I didn't want to go home.

By the time I left for college, my family's level of dysfunction had reached an all-time high (or should that be all-time low). I was so relieved and proud to get out of my house. I felt like I had parachuted out of a plane that was headed toward a fiery crash, and I had no desire to climb back into that. Maybe Tommy had no desire to go back where he came from either. Either that or he just loved football a lot more than I did.

Either way, we were both back at the track the next morning at 6 a.m. sharp. This time, the coach didn't holler out the splits the way he had been doing as we made our way around the track. Instead, he waited until we were churning our way down the homestretch and started a countdown, "5 . . . 4 . . . 3 . . . 2 . . . 1." We made it across the finish line before he ever got a chance to get to zero. I've always suspected that he probably never even started his watch. Mercy!

I spent two years "on" the Furman football team. Though I never dressed for any varsity football games, I'm glad that I never got "run off" and proud of the way I represented myself. I earned a reputation as a hard-nosed practice player who was never afraid to go full-speed into much larger, faster players. When my current students find out I played college football, they are always shocked. I usually ask them, "You remember the movie about that guy, Rudy? Well, I was *almost* as good as him."

My next running memory was also in college after my unremarkable two-year stint on the football team. This time, I found myself talked into a five-mile run with a kid we called "Preacher John." John was tall, thin, Southern and very Baptist. His dad was a preacher, and he was destined to be one as well. Something about the way he talked about his love for running made me want to join him one morning for his daily run. We jogged around the campus and parts of the adjoining neighborhoods while he alternated talking about his love for running and Jesus. He was so positive about everything and so genuine that he could get away with this kind of talk without turning people off. I actually enjoyed all but the final mile of the run, but it was days before my legs fully recovered.

In my senior year of college, I met yet a third life-changing coach that would help define me, Dr. Sandor Molnar. His students had given him the nickname (or did he give it to himself?) "The Optimal Man." In our P.E. class, he taught us about the Greek ideal of the optimal man. He referred to it as the "Triad of Human Fitness." To be a fully functioning human, he taught, one must work simultaneously and with equal vigor on the physical, the intellectual, and the social components of one's nature. Like The Great Malenko and "Wild Bill" Minahan, he was passionately enthusiastic about his work.

Dr. Molnar was a seemingly perfect prototype of all three kinds of fitness he was teaching us about. He had run several marathons, written books, and he was one of the most well-loved, socially-connected people I had ever met. Sadly, Sandor Molnar died of a brain tumor in 1987, but not before inspiring me and hundreds of others to strive toward the "optimal" life.

My wife Linda and I were inspired to start jogging together as a result of taking Dr. Molnar's personal fitness course. When we moved to Tampa after graduating from Furman in 1982, we started a routine that included running to nearby Al Lopez Park from our apartment. In the fall of that year, my best friend from high school and former Furman classmate, Mike Perez, decided to run a marathon in Atlanta where he was living. I remember going to visit him afterwards and seeing a picture on his refrigerator of him running that marathon. I was in complete awe and filled with envy of what he did. Mike and I have always been very competitive with each other in everything from golf to bowling, fishing and even girls.

Listening to him pontificate about how he handled those 26.2 miles stirred my competitive juices. At least I wasn't crazy enough to challenge him in a marathon. Instead, we decided to race each other at the Gasparilla Distance Classic 15K the next February in Tampa. When I got back to Tampa, I increased my running with the intention of beating my best friend in a 15K race. I had never run that far (9.3 miles) in my life, but that didn't matter. He might be able to run a marathon, I thought, but he's not going to come here and beat me in the Gasparilla race. It was about that time that Linda stopped running with me. I think it started getting too serious for her.

Instead, I started training with Terry Daly, another close high school friend who went to Jesuit and Furman with us. Like me, he really wanted to beat Mike. Unlike Mike and me, Terry actually had the classic ectomorphic build that so many good runners have. He also had some experience running competitively in high school. We trained for about one month. We gradually built up our endurance by trying to increase our distance with each run until we were confident we could run the 9.3-mile distance on race day. We had no idea about pacing. Instead, we just ran each run as if we were in a race. The final stretch always evolved into a macho sprint to the finish.

The three of us started the 1983 Gasparilla Distance Classic 15K together and stayed that way until about mile six. At that point, Mike dropped off of the pace. He had not kept up his training after his successful marathon debut, but at least he showed up to take his beating. Now it was down to Terry and me (and a few hundred runners ahead of us, of course).

The 1983 Gasparilla race started and finished in downtown Tampa. The majority of the course went out and back along Tampa Bay on Bayshore Boulevard. Both Terry and I finished the Bayshore section of the race together and headed into downtown Tampa side-by-side (briefly) for the final half-mile of the race. It was just before the turn onto Ashley Street where Terry left me and accelerated to the finish line. My time was actually pretty good for a beginner—just over 68 minutes (about 7:20/mile).

It wasn't enough for us to beat Mike in the Gasparilla 15K that year. He still had it over us that he had run 26.2 miles that fall in a time of 3 hours and 40 minutes. That became our new focus. Atlanta Marathon, November 1983—sub 3:40. We significantly upped our training once more. Back then, I knew NOTHING about how to train for a marathon. I had not read my first book on the subject, and, true to my youthful immaturity, I really didn't see the need to. Instead, we just kept trying to go longer and faster every time we went out for a run.

When Terry and I drove up to Atlanta that November, Mike had already moved to take a job in South Carolina so we were on our own. We picked up our registration packets and drove the course as it was illustrated in the map we were provided. That might have been a mistake. As we drove the course, one thing jumped out at both of us that neither of us had counted on—hills! Relative to our very flat training we did in Tampa, this course was a virtual rollercoaster. Then it came time to get dinner. Someone had told us that marathon runners were supposed to "carbo-load" before races, so we went to a buffet style restaurant and loaded up on bread and potatoes.

Another bit of information we were lacking regarded proper attire. I don't remember what Terry was wearing, but I decided I wanted to represent my old high school back in Tampa where I was now serving as a volunteer junior varsity football coach. I wore a grey, cotton t-shirt with "Jesuit" written in blue on the front. The shirt got me two things—some shout-outs along the course from people who obviously had some connection to a Jesuit school somewhere and two bloody nipples.

Terry and I were very fit for that race. I remember hitting the 10-mile mark in just over 70 minutes. We were flying along at nearly seven minutes per mile, well below the pace we had run for the 9.3-mile race nine months prior. It really didn't feel that bad. Just before the halfway mark, I had to stop to go to the bathroom, and not just to urinate. By the time I got out of the porta-potty, the cool air had stiffened my legs. Terry was long gone, so I tried to ease my way back into it. I was moving slower, but I felt good about the pace and my legs started to warm back up. When I reached the 20-mile mark, I started thinking about all of the hoopla I had heard from Mike and other marathoners about "the wall." Shortly after that, the course went under an overpass. On either side of the overpass, the sides were fortified with large stones—making it look like a huge wall.

Though I didn't know anyone around me, I joked aloud something like, "Hey, look. There's the wall we heard so much about. It's not that bad." It was as if the marathon gods heard my mockery and immediately struck me with what felt like rigor mortis in my legs. Both legs soon got very stiff, and they started to feel like lead weights.

Eventually, both of my legs started to cramp, and I had to walk. I stopped to stretch, walked a bit, ran slowly for a while, and then my legs cramped back up. I did this routine over and over. Each time, the walking got longer and the jogging got slower. Finally, mercifully, I could see the finish line in the distance. I tried desperately to get my form back so that I could run proudly across the finish line of my first marathon, but there was no way.

I jogged wearily across the finish line and was barely aware of the volunteers cheerfully greeting us and putting medals around our necks. I couldn't wait to get off my feet, so I walked over to some concrete steps and carefully lowered my butt to the ground. My legs continued to cramp—sometimes one leg and sometimes both legs at the same time, forcing me to lean way back and try to straighten them back out.

"Never again," I said once I got home to anyone who asked how the marathon went. I concluded that I just wasn't built for running. My thick legs and stocky physique made me too heavy to be a distance runner. I went back to racquetball, which was a sport I played avidly in college after leaving the football team. I had no appreciation back then that my Atlanta Marathon time of 3:52 was actually a pretty darn good time for a first-time marathoner. All I knew was Mike ran 12 minutes faster the previous year, and that made me a loser.

It was nearly two years before I ever ran a single step again.

Hey, I was small, but I was slow . . .

Chapter Three

BOSTON OR BUST

Sometime in the fall of 1985, I took my first jogging steps since the 1983 Atlanta Marathon. I simply had to. When my wife was pregnant with our daughter Melody, she naturally gained weight with her pregnancy. Like a good, sympathetic husband, I gained weight right along with her. She delivered a child. I just stayed fat. Once, during a trip to the grocery store when Melody was just a few months old, I weighed myself on the scale near the exit (why do they put those there?)—205 lbs.!

During my football days, I weighed about 185 lbs. When I took Dr. Sandor Molnar's P.E. class during my senior year of college, he helped us calculate our optimal weight by using a formula consisting mainly of height and body density. According to his formula, my optimal weight was supposed to be about 170 lbs. Even during my fittest marathon training periods I've never weighed less than about 174 lbs., so I have my doubts about Dr. Molnar's calculus. But I didn't need any formula to tell me that 205 lbs. was way more than "optimal" for me. My fitness was gone, and I felt pathetic. It was as if I had morphed in into an adult-size version of the doughy little boy I was before I met The Great Malenko.

With the exception of the months of training I did with Terry Daly preparing for the 1983 Atlanta Marathon, the majority of the exercise I got after giving up college football came from racquetball. I dabbled in the sport back in Tampa before ever going to Furman, but once I no longer had to worry about showing up for football workouts, I dove into racquetball full-force during my last two years at Furman. It was a popular sport among our P.E. professors and, of course, Dr. Molnar, who was one of my favorite playing partners.

Like so many things I've gotten into in my life, it became an obsession. I began travelling to tournaments all over South Carolina, and I even organized intramural tournaments on campus. At first, it provided great exercise. Eventually, I reached a level of play such that I really didn't need to do that much running. In fact, I can recall a number of elite players I met during those days who were quite overweight. The court just isn't that big, and once you learn all the angles, you can greatly reduce unnecessary running.

When Linda and I moved to Tampa after college, we moved into an apartment complex that featured racquetball courts. I was on them nearly every day. I went to work part-time for two different racquet clubs, simply to get the free court time on more quality surfaces than the ones at our apartment complex. I was also able to make some extra income giving lessons, and I traveled all over Florida to compete in tournaments. I finally developed a sciatic condition in my lower back that made playing racquetball quite painful. My playing time slowly dropped, and my weight went steadily up.

By the time I started jogging again, I was so out of shape I literally had trouble finishing one mile without taking a walking break. At 25 years old, I was clearly in the worst condition I had ever been in my life. Even when I went for my first jog with Uncle Mandy at age 10, I was more fit than that.

I took a large piece of poster board and used a marker to make a calendar-grid with three months-worth of squares. Each square was a day, and each day was a workout of some kind. Intuitively, I knew to start filling in the workouts from the polar ends. In other words, I knew where I was, and I knew where I wanted to go. I was also smart enough not to start thinking marathon again (not yet, anyway). For some reason, I wisely decided it would be enough to make it back to half of a marathon—13.1 miles. It turns out I was ahead of my time. These days, the half-marathon has actually become the fastest growing race distance.

Once I had the beginning and the end of the calendar days filled in, the rest was simple—just gradually progress in equal increments from point A (where I was) to point B (where I wanted to be). The funny thing is, after more than 25 years of experience, reading, and going to coaching clinics, that same progressive training philosophy is essentially the one I use today when designing programs for my runners.

I was even smart enough to alternate running days with other forms of training—mostly stretching, push-ups and sit-ups. After each workout, I would go straight to the poster, which I had prominently displayed in our bedroom, and put a big "X" over the completed assignment. The miles grew, and the pounds dropped. When I set out to do the final 13.1-mile run on my program, I designed a route that would take me by the school where Linda was working. She arranged to have her class outside carrying signs cheering me as I ran by. It was great.

Shortly thereafter, some friends convinced me to run in a 5K race with them and I remember thinking that 5K seemed like an awfully short distance for a race. In retrospect, my introduction to running was backwards compared to most people who enter the sport. Typically, runners start out doing 5Ks and gradually build up to longer distances. That actually makes a lot more sense. My first race had been the Gasparilla 15K, and my second was a full-blown marathon. That's just crazy.

My goal was to average 7 minutes per mile in that first 5K race. Don't ask me where I got that number. I came close, but I ended up finishing in just over 22 minutes, and immediately my next running goal was set—I was going to run a 5K under 20 minutes. I realized there were a few people my age in most 5Ks who ran under 20 minutes and earned age-group awards, and a lot of people who couldn't. It was obvious which group I wanted to belong to.

In 1986, I took a job teaching social studies and coaching football at Middleton Junior High. The inner-city public school was a dramatic change from the private, suburban middle school where I began my teaching career after graduating from Furman. In those days, public junior highs had football teams, and this job came with an opportunity to be the defensive coordinator, an important step toward my goal at the time, which was to become a head football coach—preferably at Jesuit.

All my life, I have gone back and forth between describing myself on application forms as either "white" or "Hispanic." I never felt more white in my life than the two years I worked as a teacher and coach at Middleton. In fact, it's fair to say that I was hired precisely because I WAS white—or at least NOT black. Before you start suspecting racism, think more along the lines of "reverse affirmative action." The principal who hired me was a strong, black leader named Sam Brown. Mr. Brown was part preacher, part professor and very committed to his inner-city junior high school which was once an all-black high school before integration.

"We can't get any of the white kids to come out for football," he told me in his booming tone during my interview. "Maybe if I get you out there, they can see a white face when they look at our coaching staff and feel more welcome."

Sure enough, I was the only coach who wasn't black (does that make me white?), and, strangely, the only coach that didn't smoke cigarettes. Other than all the smoking, which made our planning meetings dreadful for me, I really enjoyed teaching and coaching there. In my two years on their coaching staff, however, only one white kid ever joined our team. Maybe I wasn't white enough? The lone white kid ended up playing quarterback for us. No one ever mentioned it, but given the history of black athletes not being allowed to play quarterback because of racial stereotypes, it was an uncomfortable irony for me.

When I was starting my second year at Middleton in 1987, a new social studies teacher arrived who I soon discovered was an accomplished runner. Lynn Gray introduced me to the wonderful world of running literature. Up to this point, I had no idea that this running thing actually had basic principles and techniques like every other sport. I had seen running magazines, but I didn't realize that there was so much more substantial information and inspiration out there.

When Lynn loaned me her copy of George Sheehan's *Running and Being*, it was the first book I had ever seen that was entirely dedicated to the sport of running. To this day, I consider that book to be one of the greatest running books of all time. Dr. George Sheehan was part physician, part philosopher and all runner. His book, and later his essays in *Runner's World* magazine, gave me the words to describe what was happening to me when I ran.

Another thing I got from reading Sheehan's book was a strong desire to qualify for and run in the Boston Marathon. Sheehan dedicated a whole chapter in his book to describing the mystical allure of the world's oldest marathon and one of the most prestigious road races of all time. For every other race, all you had to do was sign the race form and pay the entry fee. Here was a race that you actually had to qualify for. Never mind that my only marathon experience was nowhere near fast enough for men my age to qualify. In my mind, qualifying for Boston was the only way for me to be considered a legitimate distance runner, and I was determined to do it.

The next book that Lynn loaned me was *The Self-Coached Runner* by Allan Lawrence and Mark Scheid. In their book, they offer programs designed to achieve specific goals for specific distances. Their approach reminded me of what I had intuitively already discovered about how to achieve a goal—gradually progressing from point A (where you are) to point B (where you want to be). I absolutely loved it. Among other things, they used scientific data to predict finishing times for longer distances based on results from shorter distances.

According to Lawrence and Scheid, if I could break 20 minutes for a 5K, I was ready to train for a 3:15 marathon. Since I was now getting close to my 20-minute 5K goal, I liked the sound of that. The Boston Athletic Association had adjusted the qualifying standards such that, when I turned 30 in 1990, I would "merely" need a 3:10 to qualify. At age 27, I wisely gave myself a couple of years before trying to run a qualifying marathon. I would learn later (the hard way) that I foolishly put too much faith in those race time conversion tables. As I mentioned earlier, it wasn't until 2000 when, after a decade of painful failures, I finally qualified for Boston.

By that time, at age 39, the qualifying standard for the Boston Marathon was a more merciful 3:20. When I finally crossed the finish line of the 2000 Clearwater Beach Marathon and saw 3:17 on the clock, I broke down in tears. There were so many times during all those years of futile planning and preparation when I thought of giving up on making it into the Boston Marathon. The way my body broke down during some of those failed attempts made me wonder if I was physically capable of meeting the standard. But every time somebody even hinted that I might not be able to qualify for Boston, it only made me more determined to prove them wrong. I worried how much more I would have to hurt to run faster. But on that January day over 12 years ago, I learned that good marathons hurt much less than bad ones—and for less time.

I learned plenty of valuable lessons during my decade-long quest to qualify for Boston, and the single biggest tip I can give somebody just getting into marathons is the long run. The weekly long run is, by far, the most important element of marathon training.

There are adaptations that your body is forced to make when you run continuously for that length of time that can't be obtained by just running steady miles every day. The question is, "How long does that run need to be?" Over my years of marathon training, I have gone back and forth on this. On one hand, if you don't practice going at or near the marathon distance, what makes you think you will be able to do it on race day? On the other hand, if you go the whole marathon distance in practice, you beat yourself up and use up resources that you will need on race day.

My experiences training for and racing marathons tell me that my goal distance for the long run should be a length that requires me to be on my feet running for about as long as I plan to be running during the marathon. For example, I used to consider 3 hours and 30 minutes to be a reasonable marathon goal most of the time. To practice for that, I would plan at least one long run that took at least 3:30.

The problem is pace. Running a 3:30-marathon requires someone to average about 8 minutes per mile. There is no way that one can or should try to run their race pace for the entire duration of their long run. In my opinion, long runs should be done at a pace that is between 30 to 60 seconds per mile slower than the anticipated marathon race pace. When I was aiming for a 3:30 hour marathon, this meant doing a long run that covered up to 24 miles, averaging about 8:30 to 9:00 per mile. This run would take about the same time (3:30) as the marathon to complete. That's about the longest training run I've ever done or would ever recommend, and it would usually be done only once in the training at least three weeks prior to the marathon.

When I have written marathon training programs for friends attempting to run their first marathon, I have never recommended a long run over 20 miles. Sometimes I have even suggested a maximum of 18 miles for the beginner. This is because most new marathoners are interested mainly in finishing the race, not necessarily racing for a time. From what I have read and seen, the average time these days for completing a marathon is about 4:30 for men and around 5:10 for women. My formula would require the average runner to do a practice run of four and a half to five hours, which is unwise. In fact, it's probably unwise for any runner to run longer than three and a half to four hours in any practice run with the possible exception of ultra-marathon training.

Elite runners will sometimes run their long training runs even closer to race pace. Most of them have the genetic attributes and years of gradual callousing to keep them from getting too beat up by these extended quality efforts. They also tend to be able to recover better, and often have the advantage of an elite runner's lifestyle, including regular recovery therapies like ice-soaking and massage. When my team is at running camp in North Carolina, for example, I have found that I can push them harder, yet they still recover faster because we have the time and resources to recover properly and regularly.

Two other kinds of long runs that have proven effective for me in marathon training are the long-pace run and the long-tempo run. In the long-pace run, I would run my marathon pace for about 13 to 15 miles to get my body accustomed to moving at that rhythm. I think you can get away with doing it five to ten seconds slower than marathon pace, since it always feels a little easier on race day with all of the adrenaline. For the long tempo-run, I would run 20 to 30 seconds per mile faster than race pace for about 8 to 10 miles. This makes your marathon pace feel that much easier on race day.

All of this brings me to the following questions: Where am I now, fitness-wise? What is my goal for the 2012 ING Miami Marathon? Is it reasonable to assume that I can still qualify for Boston? The current standard for my age group (50-54) is 3:35. Do I even want to try to run that time?

It didn't take me long to answer that last question. I don't. I've "been there and done that." I've got some cool t-shirts and even a jacket to show for it. Qualifying for Boston meant proving something to myself—and others. I'm not sure exactly what I was trying to prove, but it's been done. Miami is not about "proving" as much as it is about "doing." I want to "do" this thing because, somehow, I know it will make me happier in the end. Not "happy" like I'm going to be dancing and singing, but happy in a much deeper sense that it can help me transform my life into something better.

I have never run a marathon slower than four hours. Even my first experience in Atlanta that I thought was a failure at the time was well under four hours. To be honest, I would be very happy to keep my streak of sub 4:00 marathons unbroken. This will require a pace of about 9 minutes per mile. If I used the formula above for calculating the optimal distance for the longest run during training, this would mean averaging 9:30 per mile for a distance of about 24 miles at least once during my training. I don't think I want to run that far in training this time (or any time in the future), so it might be time to come up with a new formula. My plan for now is to wait and see how my long runs naturally progress.

If marathon running has taught me anything, it's patience . . . and humility.

Chapter Four

WHAT IT TAKES

It's time to start meeting for summer training with my cross country team. We took four weeks off from team workouts after the spring track season ended. Most of the boys have already started running some on their own in preparation for the start of summer practice. I usually plan to start our summer training exactly 24 weeks prior to the State Meet. Summer running is a must for teams or individuals who want to have any chance to compete for a title in November at the State Meet. Even though our races are only 5K, the most critical factor in the equation of success in cross country is aerobic strength (stamina and endurance), and that is best achieved by running lots of miles.

Speed helps, but in a race that is going to take most boys between 16 to 20 minutes, the runners who can hold a competitive pace over the varied terrain of a cross country course are going to have the best chance to finish up front at the end of a grueling race.

"He can't out-sprint you at the finish line if he can't keep up with you for three miles," I often remind my runners.

The summer plan is always simple. Start off running mostly easy miles and gradually increase the weekly mileage from about 50 percent less than last year's maximum to about 20 to 25 percent more than last year's peak. Generally speaking, most of our freshman work their way up to about 30 miles per week, sophomores get to 40, juniors to 50 and, if they have been injury free for three years, some seniors will get upwards of 60 miles per week by summer's end. We throw in some limited speed work during the summer, like doing short, fast "strides" on a grass field, but other than that and a lot of Ultimate Frisbee, it's mainly about the miles.

In July, I start timing some of their runs as I introduce them to "steady-state" running, which is about one minute slower than current 5K race pace. A typical mid-summer "steady-state" workout for our varsity group would be a 6-mile run in 40 minutes (about 6:40/mile). By summer's end, these "steady-state" runs evolve into "tempo" runs, which are run between 30 to 40 seconds slower than current 5K race pace. I usually aim to get our varsity group up to a 4-mile run in 24 minutes (6:00/mile) before school starts.

The hardest part is keeping the boys motivated enough to hold this steady grind through the dog days of our Florida summer. Harder still is keeping them running while they travel with their families all over the world for vacations, college visits and every other kind of getaway that many middle and upper class teenage boys tend to take when school is out. Without support and encouragement from parents, it's nearly impossible for the boys to keep up with their summer mileage. This is one of the main themes I will cover at the parent meeting I hold every June. It's hard enough for adults to maintain their training when they travel to different places. Kids have much less control over their surroundings and really need their parents' help to make running possible sometimes.

Some parents try too hard to help their kids with their running during the summer. Today's parents are very accustomed to hiring tutors and private coaches to give their children every advantage in the classroom and on the playing field. For many sports, like baseball, golf, tennis or soccer, it probably makes good sense. If you can afford it, a private coach can focus individual attention on the athlete and teach successful techniques and fundamentals that will improve performance.

For distance runners, it can sometimes be counterproductive, especially if the private coach is not communicating and cooperating with the team coach. It would be like being treated by two doctors for the same problem, and taking two different medicine treatments—one from each doctor. Each treatment might be effective on its own, but together they might actually be harmful. Private running coaches usually focus on speed. Speed-work has a place in our training cycle, but too much in the summer interferes with our year-round cycle and increases the risk of injuries.

Some parents like to put their kids in summer 5K races. Either they think that racing during the summer will make them better in the fall, or they just like to see (and let others see) their kids win trophies. Kids who race or do lots of speed-work in the summer tend to start off the season looking strong, and then fade when it counts in November.

This year's team has the potential to be the best in the five years that I have been at Plant High School. We have five seniors returning with varsity experience, plus one new senior who joined last winter and ran varsity times on the track in the spring. Additionally, we have six returning runners who have demonstrated the ability to be competitive varsity scorers. In my experience, any boy who runs under 5 minutes for one mile, 11 minutes for two miles, or 18 minutes for a 5K in the spring, has a chance to be a competitive varsity runner the next fall. In order to travel in late July to our varsity running camp in Boone, North Carolina, a runner must achieve at least one of those three time standards before the end of track season. This summer we will have 12 boys making that trip.

Our team competes in 4-A, which is Florida's largest classification based on school population size. These days, a team needs to have at least five runners who can run a 5K under 17 minutes to have any chance to compete for a state title. The most important runner on a cross country team is very often the fifth man. That's because of the way our meets are scored. Each of the top five runners adds to his team's score by his place in the race. For example, first place equals one point, and 50th place equals 50 points. A team's score is calculated by adding the places of the top five runners, and the team with the lowest score wins the meet. So the team whose fifth runner crosses the line first often has the best chance to win, versus another team whose top runner took first place in the race, but their fifth runner was 100 places back.

In the final stages of the 2004 State Meet, our team from Tampa Jesuit, where I was coaching at the time, and the Belen Jesuit team from Miami each had four runners safely in the finish chute. My quick calculations indicated we had a narrow lead, but the team score was very close. Whichever team got their fifth runner in first was likely going to be the state champion.

All eyes (especially mine) stared intently down towards the final turn to see if the next uniform color would be blue (us) or yellow (them). Just then, a small blue figure made the turn and started the sprint to the finish. Surprisingly, it wasn't the blue figure I expected. Instead of our normal fifth or sixth man, it was Ian, our usual seventh man, whom I had almost replaced on the roster because of his poor performance at the previous week's region meet.

I waited a few seconds to make sure no yellow jerseys were in close pursuit. There were none. Then I started a mad sprint toward the finish area to be as close as possible to the scene of our impending victory. As I did this, I noticed another (not so small) blue figure in the spectator area. It was Ian's dad.

"He did it! He did it! He did it!" I was screaming as I veered towards Ian's dad, who was beaming with pride. When he got within reach, I extended both of my hands towards his chest. My hands clutched the front of his shirt on either side of his upper chest, and I tried to pull him toward me and shake him with excitement. Instead, when I pulled my hands toward me I ripped his shirt right off of his chest. Embarrassed, but still intent on getting to the finish area to see my team, I handed him the shredded remains of his shirt and sprinted away.

Seven years later, Linda gave me a surprise party to celebrate my induction into the Florida Athletic Coaches Hall of Fame. The meeting hall was filled with over 100 former runners and parents, some of whom were kind enough to get up and share their favorite memories from our time together. Ian's dad got up and gave his version of that story, much to everyone's amusement. Then he gave me a gift. When I opened it, I was pleasantly surprised to find the shredded blue shirt which I had ripped off of his chest on that magical night.

My current runners at Plant High School have never experienced that kind of magic, so I recently invited next year's seniors over to my house for pizza, and I shared some of these championship memories with them. The girls' cross country team has won nine state championships including last season, but the Plant boys have never won a state title.

A big part of winning is believing you can win and eventually expecting to win. Once we won our first state title at Jesuit in 1998, it was never as hard to convince our future teams that they could win. Banners and pictures were always constant reminders of the legacy handed down by former Jesuit runners. A championship mentality eventually developed. Our Plant girls' team has that championship mentality. They believe they can win. Our boys don't. They might "say" they believe, but I can tell the difference, and that's been a source of great frustration for me since I started coaching at Plant five years ago.

On one hand, we have been getting better almost every year. Our average team times have steadily gotten faster since my first year at Plant, and three out of those four years our top runner has set a new school record for 5K. On the other hand, our team finish at the state meet has not improved. Since I started at Plant, our teams have finished fourth, then sixth, then a very disappointing eleventh, and last year we finished seventh. What bothers me most is that we haven't even been in the hunt.

It's true that my Jesuit teams competed in 2-A (smaller school class) while my Plant teams were 3-A until 2008 and 4-A since, but that's no consolation for me. My competitors are coaching at large schools, but so am I. The reason that these classes exist in the first place is to level the playing field. In a level playing field, my coaching competitors are getting more out of their teams than I am.

School size doesn't mean that much in cross country anyway. For example, next season the best returning team in any classification is the Belen Jesuit team which is one of the smallest 3-A schools, and they were 2-A during my time at Jesuit. The real reason that my teams have been unable to compete for a title is that there has been a tremendous growth in our sport since the 1990s, and the top runners and teams have gotten significantly better.

When I started coaching cross country in 1995, less than 40 boys covered the 3-mile state meet course under 16 minutes. Last year, nearly 50 boys finished the 5K course (about 170 meters longer) under 16 minutes. Running 16 minutes for 5K is the equivalent to running 3 miles in 15:30. Less than 10 boys ran the 3 mile state course under 15:30 in 1995. What was once very good is now closer to average. What was once good enough to win is no longer good enough to even have a chance.

Simply put, there are more coaches pushing more kids to run more miles than when we started winning titles at Jesuit. Those days, about 40 miles per week was pretty standard for many elite boys' teams. These days my team is competing against several programs that are running 60 to 70 miles per week. This is actually more of a renaissance than an innovation. From the time I started coaching, I have heard stories of how much more boys were running in the 1970s and early 1980s. The numbers bear out that truth. Distance running times across the country during that period were significantly faster than in the 1990s and early 2000s. Many coaches in the 1990s rationalized that we were running fewer, but "smarter" miles. The idea was that we replaced long, easier running with faster interval training and far less overall mileage. The arguments on each side were never-ending, but the results speak for themselves.

I've slowly increased the amount of running I ask my boys to do since I've been at Plant. This probably explains why we've gotten a bit faster each year. Still, it doesn't seem to be enough to catch the top programs in the state. Two years ago our team was ravaged by injuries, and I started getting scared to push the boys. By the end of the season I had backed off on mileage and intensity so much that the boys who were not injured lacked the fitness to compete at their peak. This was the main reason for our 11th place finish that year.

This rash of injuries made me seriously rethink just how much mileage was prudent. But the more I talked to other coaches of successful teams, I came to the conclusion that we had just been the victims of some bad luck. We do most of our miles on grass and dirt trails, which are softer and create less stress on shins and joints. A few of the high mileage programs in our state (especially in the Miami area) do nearly all of their running on roads and sidewalks, which is commonly thought to result in more stress injuries. Moreover, the intensity of our running didn't seem to be as high as some of these higher mileage programs. They were running farther and faster than us with fewer injuries.

As in football or any other sport, injuries are part of the game. During my time as a football player and later a coach, I learned the paradoxical truth that you can actually increase risk of injury by playing scared and not going full-speed. I hate to see any athlete suffer an injury, but if you start getting scared of getting hurt, you lose your edge to train and compete at the highest level. I had gotten scared and lost my edge. I was also just stubbornly repeating what worked in the past. If the challenge has gotten harder, so must our training.

So this year's team is going to run farther and faster than any team in the history of Plant cross country (at least since I've been the coach). Given the number and quality of veteran runners we have, I expect the best season ever. As I study the teams returning for next season, there are two programs in class 4-A that will return next fall with significantly better squads than we will. Colonial High School from Orlando beat us handily in the region meet last year, and they return all but one of their top runners. They will be the preseason number one team in our classification. Miami Columbus has won the 4-A State Meet three years in a row, and, though they graduated most of last year's top runners, they are still deep enough to return more elite runners than we do. Five or six other teams will return squads similar to ours.

It is a formidable challenge for us to improve enough to get to the level that these two teams already seem to be. And, even if we do get there, where will they be by then? Still, there is a long way to go for them and us. Anything can happen. Kids move in, and kids move out. Kids get hurt, and kids make unexpected quantum leaps. It's not as predictable as some might think. If we can do the work I have planned, stay healthy and compete with courage, I will be happy.

Well, sort of. There's nothing like winning.

Chapter Five
A QUIET HOUSE

May 2011

The first month of my marathon training is over. I logged 101 miles in the month of May, which is right on the pace I planned. In June, I hope to log about 115 miles. If I continue to increase by about 15 miles each month, I will reach 200 miles per month by December. December and January are my two favorite months to run, and that's when I plan to hold my peak mileage for about eight weeks before tapering for the race in late January. I love running in the cool, Florida winter weather, and my school schedule is at its lightest during that time since I am between cross country and track seasons.

The other important training progression is the weekly long run. I have done four 8-mile runs in the past five weeks. This month, my weekly long runs should average 10 miles. Again, if I continue this slow, steady progression, I should be up to 20-mile long runs by November.

I also went to my doctor for a thorough physical exam last month. It's a good idea to get checked out when you begin a major physical endeavor like this, but that's not the only reason I did it. About six weeks ago, I started having some mild soreness in my chest. Common sense told me that I had hurt myself when I was demonstrating some strength drills to our younger runners. But given my family history (and Linda's urging), I thought it was best to get a thorough check up. After doing all sorts of tests on me, the doctors seem certain my heart is fine, and the soreness was from either muscle or cartilage inflammation.

Both my primary doctor and the cardiologist remarked about my high level of fitness. My resting pulse is 58 and my blood pressure is lower than normal. Both are signs that my cardiovascular system is very strong. My other health markers like blood sugar, cholesterol, etc. were excellent also. Even considering all of this, I'm pretty sure I will still have heart trouble one day. As much as we can improve our chances of avoiding or surviving heart attacks with our lifestyle choices, genetics are impossible to overcome completely. My grandfather had a stroke in his 60s and eventually died of a heart attack. My father had a major heart attack at 55, which he survived, and then another in his sleep at 65, which he did not. And my older brother died from a heart attack before he was my age.

All three of them smoked, and my brother was also overweight with high blood pressure. I have never smoked. I tried to drink when I was in college like so many other kids, but I've always had an aversion to alcohol. I just couldn't drink it. Only in the past 10 years have Linda and I started enjoying some occasional wine with dinner. I suppose it was a good thing that I couldn't drink, since my mother struggled with alcoholism for most of her life and died in her mid-50s as a result of damage to her liver. Maybe my aversion was at least partially conditioned by the association of alcohol and the anguish it brought to our family.

Maybe it's just luck. The bottom line is I know that all of my running won't keep me from having a heart attack if I am genetically predisposed to have one. Running may not extend my life one second more than I was destined to live. And I don't really care. If I do live longer because I run, that will be a bonus. I run because I love running, and running loves me back. The days, weeks and years that I live are happier because I am healthier, and I am healthier because I run.

Running touches all of the components of the "triad of human fitness" that Sandor Molnar taught. Not only does running help me feel better physically and emotionally, but I believe I think better because of my running. There are scientific studies that show a positive correlation between running and intelligence. Are smart people more likely to run, or does running actually make you smarter? A recent article in the *The New York Times Magazine* (April 22, 2012) by Gretchen Reynolds cited studies which suggest that the latter might be true. Rats that ran regularly in these tests outperformed the non-running control group on memory tests.

There are related factors like patience, endurance and discipline that positively correlate with both intelligence and running. For example, the majority of the kids who come out for cross country are already some of the best students even before they run a single step because they possess genetic and environmental factors

for his amusement). He fell head-over-heals in love with running, especially the marathon. He joined me in my quest to qualify for Boston. In the beginning of his training, he struggled to keep up with me. Before long, I could no longer keep up with him in marathons, and he was running two or three for every one that I ran.

Greg made the same dramatic progress as a coach. He is far more competitive than he appears, and he became as obsessed as I was with creating new plans and strategies to make our team better. When I moved to Plant High School in 2007, he became the head cross country coach at Jesuit, and he has done a great job keeping up the winning tradition we started together. Greg's teams have finished in the top three all but one of the past four years. He likes to tell people that we never won a cross country state championship at Jesuit until he started coaching. We won our first of four cross country titles in 1998, the year he joined us.

But more than all of those victories, the thousands of miles we've logged together forged a friendship that has had a profound effect on my life. The fact that Greg and I were opposites (at least seemingly) was a good thing for me. His low-key approach to athletics helped me evolve out of my do-or-die football mentality into a mindset more suitable to coaching runners and more healthy for my life in general.

Whenever people ask me if I miss Jesuit, my response is always, "I miss my friends." It was difficult, especially my first year after leaving, to adjust to not seeing the same familiar faces every day. Happily, Greg and I continued our tradition of running together nearly every Sunday. The best part of those runs is always the coffee stop we make on the way home. At first it was 7-11, then Dunkin' Donuts and eventually the beloved Starbucks. Each of our running locations now has its own Starbucks that we visit on our way home.

I was worried when I started coaching at Plant and we became competitors that these weekly running/coffee encounters would come to an end. It was somewhat awkward early on, but as time has passed, and as the runners I coached at Jesuit eventually graduated, that awkwardness has also passed. Obviously, our teams are still competitors, but since we are in different classifications, we each have our own prizes we can run for once the championship season commences in November each year.

Greg was one of the first people with whom I shared my recent re-birth as a runner and my plan to write this book. Even though he has been struggling with a hamstring injury for nearly a year, he has committed to joining me for the 2012 ING Miami Marathon. Last Sunday, he joined me for my eight-mile run in Temple Terrace. That was the longest run he has done in a year because of his injury. He had no pain in his hamstring, but now one of his knees was hurting. I am hoping that, like my own body has recently done since my knee surgery, his body will re-adapt to the stress of long distance running. This journey will mean so much more if I can share it with the Red Monkey.

*The Red Monkey and I have logged thousands of miles together
since the fall of 1998.*
(Photo courtesy of Caitlyn Boza)

Chapter Six

MY BIG FAIL

June 2011

The second month of my training for the 2012 ING Miami Marathon is over. I ran 112 miles in the month of June, which is just three miles shy of my goal of 115 miles. I could have squeezed in a three-mile run the day before I took my team up to Florida State University for a team retreat, but I chose to give myself a rest day before spending the next three days trying to run the hilly trails of Tallahassee with some pretty fit young runners. It turned out to be a good decision. I was able to run fairly comfortably with the slower of the two groups on some pretty challenging running venues. Each course we ran provided soft surfaces (mostly grass, dirt and clay), beautiful scenery and plenty of steep (for us) climbs.

The three-day trip to Tallahassee was a good way to break up the summer routine, run some quality trails and have some fun. The drive to Tallahassee is four hours each way. Unlike our big trip to North Carolina in late July, just about all of our returning runners are eligible to attend, so we had a total of 16 runners. For the younger boys, the van ride is a big part of the fun. I wisely let our team dad, Ken Mersereau, drive the van with all the sophomores. By the end of the trip, I think one more goofy comment would have sent this normally good natured man over the edge. The older kids tend to talk less. They plug in to their iPods and sleep most of the way.

We ran each morning, and we spent the rest of the time doing fun activities like Frisbee, swimming in a natural spring at a state park and bowling. Because of the abundance of incredible running trails, Tallahassee has become known to some as "Trailahassee," a name coined by Bob Braman, Florida State University's head cross country and track coach. I always make it a point to introduce my runners to Bob, who is one of the most successful college track coaches in the United States. Last season his men's team captured the ACC Championship and then went on to a runner-up finish in the NCAA National Championship Meet. As a result, the U.S. Track & Field and Cross Country Coaches Association (USTFCCCA) named FSU the winner of the John McDonnell Award, presented to the top overall men's program. Even with all of that success, Bob is the most accessible college coach I have ever met. He has become a very good friend, and he's been a great resource for all Florida high school distance coaches over the years on everything from training to meet management.

I always try to do some teaching during these trips as well. Some of the teaching is simply reminding our team how to act appropriately in various circumstances. Sometimes, I try to teach the principles of training so that they will better understand the purpose of each type of workout that we do. I usually put my most intense focus during these teaching sessions on our team goals and traditions. This year's theme is "Dream It, Plan It, Do It." I want to make sure each kid on the team knows exactly what our "dream" is, what our "plan" is to reach that dream and exactly what he must "do" to help make it happen.

Since Plant boys have never won a state championship, I shared some of my previous championship experiences to help make that possibility seem real to them. I told them about the room in my house that is dedicated to previous state champions. I explained to them that I painted one wall of that room in Vegas gold (Plant's color), so that it will one day match all of the Plant boys cross country state championship photos.

"You guys are good enough to be the first Plant team to be immortalized on that wall," I told them. We reviewed the plan for the season. I went over the remainder of the summer training schedule, and we talked about each of the races we would run. I wanted to assure them that every detail from June to November was carefully planned with one goal in mind. "There will be factors out of our control that will help determine the season's outcome," I told them, "so we have to ensure that we control every factor that we can." The most obvious factor under our control is running miles. I made sure they knew how many miles their rivals were running. Other factors under our control include getting proper rest, nutrition, even keeping up grades and discipline. "Doing the right thing in all those areas will not guarantee success," I explained, "but neglecting them can quickly end our dream."

Our team's July practice schedule should be conducive to my personal goal of running 130 miles for the month. For the next three weeks, our team will practice every Monday, Wednesday and Friday at Al Lopez Park, and every Tuesday, Thursday and Saturday we will run various trails around the Tampa area. Al Lopez is only 4.5 miles from Plant, but it also happens to be across the street from Jesuit so we often run into Greg and the Jesuit boys there. The practices at the park will include all of the incoming freshmen, and on those days my running will be limited as I focus on getting to know each one and teaching them about our program.

On the trail running days it will be just the varsity guys, and they will usually run 8 to 12 miles each time, so it should be easy for me to run 6 to 8 miles of my own without too much trouble. I will need to average about 30 miles per week to make 130 for the month. One week, Linda and I will be at a beach house in Englewood. This beach area is not well-suited for running, and it will be difficult to do 30 miles that week. On the other hand, the final week of July I will be in Boone, North Carolina, with my team at a running camp, and I am sure I can easily make up the difference under those ideal conditions.

I also need to continue my Sunday long run progression. In July, I want to average 12 miles for my long runs. In June, I did four long runs ranging from 9 to 11 miles. Two of those were 10-mile runs in Temple Terrace with Greg. He is still not back to top form, but the pain in his hamstring is nearly gone. Though still struggling with pain in his left knee, Greg is slowly improving and building his miles back up.

The 9-miler was done in Blowing Rock, North Carolina, during a short vacation that I took with Linda. That run included at least four miles of climbing some very steep trails. The highlight was a 60-foot climb up a fire tower located at the peak of that trail from which I could see beautiful views of the North Carolina mountains. I'll be back on that trail next month with my team. Happily, my legs seem to be responding better and better as the mileage slowly builds each week. Best of all, the joy of running is still growing step by step.

While we were in Blowing Rock, we stayed with Dennis Jones, my friend and mentor who first suggested I write this book, and his wife Caroline. Dennis and Caroline are treasured friends, and they were among the first set of parents of cross country runners I ever allowed myself to get close to on a social level. Their son Victor was in Andrew's class at Jesuit and also ran cross country.

Having my own son on the team changed my perspective on coaching cross country. It made me keenly aware of how the boys responded to the rigors of training once they got home from practice, and it made me more conscious of the stresses and anxieties of the parents. Prior to Andrew joining my team, I didn't necessarily want too much contact with runners' parents. I would carefully seek out one or two trusted parents each season that could assist me with logistical matters, but I resisted most parent volunteers. Mostly, I think I was interested in maintaining complete control over the team, and I was afraid of allowing other people to assert their personal agendas into our program.

These days, a good percentage of our friends are folks whose sons ran on my cross country teams. Most of these are parents whose sons were on the team with Andrew. Though it has been over six years since Andrew graduated from Jesuit, several of these dads still contact me regularly to play golf, celebrate important events with their families and even share their vacation homes. Linda still meets monthly with a book club made up entirely of moms of my former runners.

I doubt there will ever be another group of parents with whom I bond as closely as this group, but allowing them into my life has changed me forever as a coach and a teacher. I have become more inviting and less suspicious of parents. Part of it is age too. Most of my runners' parents these days are younger than I am now. I'm sure this makes them seem less threatening. I also feel like I have some wisdom to share with them about parenthood now that I am a successful empty-nester.

On the other hand, I am still very explicit with parents about giving me room to coach during races and practices. Otherwise, many parents would feel free to come right on into our team camps just before or after races. Most parents would not think of going onto the sideline of the football game to mingle with their son and his teammates. Parents don't go into baseball dugouts and ask their boys how they are doing or if they need anything (at least not in

51

high school). Each year I assign specific parents to be on the lookout for newbie parents who start to wander over to our team area and invite those "helicopters" over to a separate parent area. Sometimes I am really clever, and I ask a parent who is a potential interference problem to do this task. It's passive-aggressive, I know, but it's effective.

I have heard and read much about how today's parents are so much more involved in the lives of their kids. The term "helicopter parent" has become an apt way to describe how some parents hover over their kids 24/7. In general, it does seem that parents are way more involved in their kids' lives than when I was growing up. Many of my most aggravating childhood memories involve being told to sit and wait while the adults finished talking or doing whatever it was they were doing. When I was a kid, the parents' agenda seemed to be focused more on the needs and wants of the adults. "Kids should be seen, not heard," the saying went.

Linda and I both remember being allowed to roam our neighborhoods freely when we were barely 10 years old. Neither of us felt neglected. It was just the way things were. Adults were busy doing what they needed and wanted to do, and we were often left to entertain ourselves. Today's parents seem to go to great lengths to conform their schedules to the needs and wants of the kids. I know that Linda and I did.

For the first 10 years of their schooling, both of our kids attended Independent Day School, where Linda was a teacher. She had each of them in her class for a year. Andrew then went on to Jesuit, where he ran on my team and studied U.S. Government in my class. He and I rode to and from school together every day for four years, and I loved it. For the most part, our friends were the parents of their friends, and our schedule was based primarily on their needs. Like anything else, involvement in your kids' lives can be taken to the extreme and become a negative thing. In general, though, I think this trend of child-centered parenting is mostly a good thing.

Some argue that it is not, citing statistics which show a growing number of twenty-somethings who are coming home to live with their parents. This "failure to launch" phenomenon can obviously be correlated with the "helicoptering" trend, but it's still too soon to determine exactly how this next generation will be affected in the long run by all this extra nurturing.

For myself, I treasure the level of relationship I have with Melody and Andrew. I enjoy a far deeper and healthier connection to my kids than either of my parents ever had with me. Each of them seems to be maturing into adulthood at a healthy pace. For sure, neither is as "far along" into adulthood as I was at their age, but who's to say that slower isn't better? What's the rush? Linda and I were married at 19, homeowners at 21 and parents at 24. Even at that pace, we too were slower to "mature" than our parents were. Mine married at 17.

Some may point to this trend of slower transition into adulthood as evidence that our society is getting weaker and softer. My tendency is to see this is a positive thing. I have great hope for the next generation. Though there are ways in which today's kids lack some of the wherewithal and common sense that previous generations obtained by their age, I am frequently amazed at the many ways in which they seem to be well-equipped to lead our society into a better tomorrow. Obviously, my students are still just kids and they often do childish things that kids do, but I'm regularly impressed by their mature concern for each other, for the environment and for the future.

As I mentioned earlier, kids are under more stress than ever before. This is partly because competition for college admission has become so intense. A student these days who has the same scores I did in high school has zero chance to get into my alma mater Furman. This is the mindset I take into my classroom every day and, I believe, why I am effective at getting students to give me their best effort. Part of it is as simple as making sure the students know that you appreciate what they are going through rather than shrugging off their distress as childish whining. Some teachers blatantly discount the real stress some of our kids are under. Some talk about kids as if they were the enemy instead of the reason we even have a job.

If a teacher has the belief that it is "us vs. them," the students quickly clue into that mindset, and it's "game-on." When I was a kid, I could be a teacher's worst nightmare if I felt that sort of antagonistic challenge. On the other hand, if I perceived a teacher to be a true advocate who cared about what I was going through, even if they were challenging me academically (like Martha Connors did), they would get my full respect and my best effort. If a teacher believes that kids today are slackers who are getting off easier than we did, it will be impossible to hide that disdain from the students, and the result will be reciprocal contempt for the teacher. I submit that many teachers who claim their students are "disrespectful" should examine the level of respect they show the kids.

I am aware that this is a rather "high horse" I'm riding, so let me confess right now that my beliefs about today's kids are largely rooted in the particularly privileged population with whom I have been blessed to work. For all but a few years of my career, the great majority of students I have taught and coached have been middle and upper-class and mostly the children of college graduates. My first teaching job was at a private middle school in one of Tampa's best neighborhoods. I then took the public school job at Middleton Junior High in one of Tampa's poorest, most crime-ridden neighborhoods, but I spent only two years there before dedicating the next 18 years Jesuit. Now I am at Plant, which is a public school, but it's located in one of Tampa's oldest and wealthiest neighborhoods and, as a result, has a disproportionate percent of its population that hardly differs from that of the local private schools.

Actually, I didn't go straight from Jesuit to Plant. I don't think I could have done that. I will try to explain why shortly. No, before I went to Plant, I spent the 2006-2007 school year digesting a big slice of "humble pie." There may be a few people reading this who are thinking or saying something to themselves like, "This guy's got a lot of nerve talking like he's such a great teacher, when all he's really done is teach the best and the brightest." There, I said it for you. Even better, if you were thinking anything like that, this next section may be your favorite part of the book so far—"my big fail."

The decision to leave Jesuit was as much about a midlife need to do something "more" with my life as anything else. It was a very difficult thing to do, if for no other reason than I had been at Jesuit for so long. I left Jesuit and went to teach at Leto High School. Over the last two decades, Leto's student population has become characterized by a disproportionate number of relatively poor, Hispanic immigrants, many of whom were still struggling to learn English. Ironically, that made leaving Jesuit easier for me (at first, anyway).

As I alluded to earlier, if I had transferred from Jesuit to Plant, it would have felt like a betrayal. Except for the fact that Jesuit is private and Plant is public, they are rival schools which have much in common. A good portion of the Jesuit student body lives in the Plant district. It was much easier for me to tell my students and colleagues at Jesuit that I was going to Leto because, in many ways, that would be living out the Jesuit motto of "Men for Others." I wasn't going to be competing with Jesuit in any way. Instead, I was going to serve "others" as we had been taught in our Jesuit training.

The offer to go teach at Leto came from one of my former high school football coaches, Dan Bonilla. Dan was a very hard-working assistant football coach who worked his way from physical education teacher to assistant principal while I was a student at Jesuit. Not long after I graduated from Jesuit, Dan left Jesuit to start a career as a public school administrator. Thanks in large part to his relentless drive to succeed, he was in his second principal position by the time I ran into him again in 2006. He planted the idea in my head of going to a public school where I could make "a real difference in kids' lives." He was not subtle when he pointed out to me that the boys I was teaching at Jesuit already had everything they needed to make it in society.

"The kids I'm working with at Leto need every bit of everything we give them to have even a fighting chance," he stated passionately.

I reflected back to the two years I worked at Middleton before going to Jesuit. I remembered that I felt very guilty about leaving those kids after only two years to go serve the more privileged private school kids. Maybe this was my chance to make that right. Shortly after my second and final interview, I was offered a job at Leto teaching economics, and I was also hired as the social studies department head.

When Dan and I talked about the position at Leto, the subject of coaching never came up. School was ending, and I had already planned the summer training and summer camps for the Jesuit boys even before my first interview at Leto. Part of me wanted to make the "clean break" with Jesuit, including the cross country program which had won consecutive state championships the previous two years. But I couldn't bring myself to let that part of Jesuit go just yet. With permission from both principals, I was able to continue coaching the Jesuit cross country team the following season.

Less than two weeks after getting hired at Leto and announcing my decision to my colleagues at Jesuit, I boarded a plane bound for New York City to help my daughter find an apartment. I took the morning newspaper onto the plane with me, and soon after take-off, I opened it up to find a shocking surprise: Dan Bonilla had been reassigned to another high school. My bold re-entry into the world of public school's most needy kids just got riskier. Luckily, my new principal was great to us and gave me as much support and encouragement as any newly hired teacher could ask for. I ended up needing a lot more support and encouragement than I ever thought I would.

It wasn't long before it dawned on me how many years had passed since I had tried to teach students who were not as prepared or motivated to learn. I had the best of intentions when I went to Leto to make the world a better place, but I grossly underestimated how difficult a transition it would be. I taught subject content at Jesuit, and I enjoyed doing it. What my new students needed more than anything were the skills with which my former students had arrived in my class already possessing. I was not equipped to give them what they needed most.

I went from feeling like an accomplished teacher to questioning my ability to teach. One good thing about our Hillsborough County School District is that there is no shortage of teacher training. At Jesuit, I basically taught myself how to be a teacher. In our school district today, teachers have ample opportunities to choose trainings that will equip them to do their jobs. I took advantage of several of these trainings, and I slowly (very slowly, it seemed) started to get some sense of how to approach this new challenge.

After the 2006 fall season, I finally gave up coaching cross country at Jesuit and decided to start coaching track at Leto that spring. I felt it was time to make this move to Leto with complete commitment. When I first started coaching track at Jesuit in 1989, Leto's distance running program was a dominant force in the state. Their coach, Bobby Ennis, won seven state titles, and his dominant

Leto distance program was referred to as the "Long Red Row." Over the years since his retirement from coaching in 1998, this storied program sunk to being one of the weakest in the county, often unable to score at meets because they lacked the minimum of five finishers in a race. This would be my new quest. I was going to resurrect the "Long Red Row."

Again, I had no real idea what I was getting into.

Before I ever took the job at Leto, I sat with Bobby Ennis on the front porch of his home and asked him directly, "Do you think it's possible for me to get Leto distance running back on top?"

"No, I don't," he replied without a moment's hesitation. This should have been the end of my pipe dream. Bobby is as good a friend and fan of mine as anyone that I know, and his knowledge of Leto is better than anyone's when it comes to this subject. But, for some crazy reason (classic hubris?), I didn't let that stop me.

I started a recruiting campaign that took me into nearly every freshman and sophomore class. I gave speeches in which I tried to quickly teach young Leto students about their school's glorious past in distance running. I passed out flyers that invited them to start training through the winter in preparation for the upcoming spring track season. I focused on recruiting boys, because that's what I already knew best, and that is where Bobby had his success at Leto.

I was able to get a small group of boys to start meeting after school when we returned from winter break in early January 2007. By the time the track season started in late February, the group had as many as eight boys. I put my heart and soul into this project. Eventually, I even put my car into it. I ended up selling my perfectly good SUV and I purchased an old, beat-up, red (Leto's color) minivan, eventually known as the "Red Rocket," from one of the custodians so that I could transport as many boys away from the campus as possible to run at parks and trails. I also convinced several of my friends (including generous former Jesuit parents) to donate money to provide training resources and travel opportunities for my new runners.

Even with all of this passionate effort, by mid-season we were down to just four boys whom I could count on to show up regularly for practice. Only one, an eager and talented freshman named Roddy, showed any real interest in being a distance runner. Late in the spring track season, the Plant team came to Leto for a dual meet. My small group held their own the best they could, but we were overwhelmed in every running event by the swarms of Plant runners. Except for their black uniforms, they reminded me of my old Jesuit teams. At one point during the meet, Plant's head track coach, Shawn Balow, came over and made what I thought was a joke at the time.

"You should come over to Plant and coach the distance runners for me," he said.

"Yeah, that would be great," I replied with a chuckle. Even though he did seem to need some help, given the overwhelming number of runners they had, I still assumed his remark was nothing more than pleasantry between coaches.

Two weeks later I got a call from the Plant football coach, Robert Weiner. Robert started teaching at Jesuit in 1988, the same year that I did. Not only did we arrive together, we also shared the same dream of being the next head football coach at Jesuit. Even though he was one of Jesuit's most popular teachers and was essentially the head coach-in-waiting when Dom Ciao retired in 2003, Robert was surprisingly passed over for a former college coach from out of town. Feeling betrayed, he left Jesuit a couple of years before I did and began teaching and coaching baseball in another county. One year later in 2004, he transferred to Plant to be the head football coach. Within four years, he coached the Panthers to their first state title in football, and they've won two more since.

"Did Shawn talk to you about coming to Plant?" he asked me when he called.

"I thought he was just kidding around," I replied. He then went on to explain that there was a social studies opening at Plant, and that Shawn, who was coaching cross country and track, wanted to switch to J.V. football in the fall. Shawn did not want to abandon the cross country team unless a qualified coach would come in and nurture the program that he had helped build. That's what gave Bob the idea to encourage me to apply for the job at Plant.

I explained that I just couldn't do it. I had made a public commitment to work with a more needy population, and I had not even been there an entire year yet. Many of my old friends from

Jesuit had even donated money to help me rebuild the Leto running program.

I hung up the phone, but the conversation continued to resonate in my mind. On one hand, it would be humiliating to give up on this new mission after such a short time, but I was growing more and more unhappy at my new job. In fact, I had even gone to a Jesuit baseball game that spring with the hope that I would run into the principal, and somehow he would urge me to come back. I did see the principal, and we chatted, but there was no invitation to return. Why should there be? I was "Mr. World Changer," out there being the ultimate "man for others." I felt truly stuck, and I started to think that maybe this Plant job might be a small window of opportunity to return to the type of work that I loved so well. When I went online to see exactly what kind of social studies vacancy they had open at Plant, it was the sign that I was hoping for—A.P. psychology!

Of all of the social studies classes I had taught over my 25-year career, psychology was clearly my favorite. When it came time to choose a master's degree program, I selected counselor education specifically because of the number of psychology classes I could take. But we only offered regular high school psychology at Jesuit, and I was hungry to go deeper. So my last two years there, I pleaded with our administration to add the college-level A.P. psychology to our curriculum, but they were unable to do so. Now I had a chance to spend the majority of my day teaching college-level psychology to some of our county's brightest students. On top of that, there was a large group of distance runners waiting for a coach to take them to the next level. I called Coach Weiner back immediately.

Luckily, the job was still available, but it would only be open for the next 48 hours. The administration had two days to fill this position or a teacher would be chosen for them by the district. I met with Plant's principal, Rob Nelson, the very next morning. On the drive back to Leto after the interview, Mr. Nelson called to offer me the job, but I was unable to accept immediately. I asked for 24 hours.

There was no doubt in my mind that I should take the job, but I had to decide if I could cope with the shame of giving up so soon after declaring publicly what I'd planned to do. Obviously, I accepted the job the next morning. Before I left Leto, I arranged for

$1,000 of money that my friends donated to be split into two college scholarships (one boy and one girl) to be offered to worthy seniors. The balance of the funds went into an account that Bobby Ennis and I had started to help Leto get a rubberized track, which the school now has.

I also assured Roddy that I would continue to be his coach as long as he wanted me to help him in his running career. For the next two years, he frequently trained with my team and became good friends with many of the Plant runners. He continued to improve, and we often saw him at meets where our boys would cheer him as if he was on our own team. In his senior year, he joined a successful running team that is associated with a running store which was more conveniently located in his neighborhood.

On one hand, it was arguably the most colossal failure of my professional life. My attempt to teach kids in real need and to resurrect a once-great running program was over in less than a year. And I had quit—which is worse than failing in my book. On the other hand, I am proud of myself for not letting my ego and pride get in the way of making a wise decision for me in the long run. I learned some valuable lessons and gained some much-needed humility. What I do know for certain is that I am a better teacher now than I ever have been in my career, that I am doing what I do best, and that I love doing what I do with all my heart.

Chapter Seven

THE FIRE TOWER

July 2011

July is over, and the dog days of summer are in full force. Even at 6 a.m. when I open my front door to get the newspaper, the hot, humid air covers my skin like a sticky, suffocating, wet blanket. It's a drastic change from the cool, dry air we enjoyed last week during our team cross country camp in Boone, North Carolina. Twelve boys, team dad Ken Mersereau and I flew to Greensboro, North Carolina, where we rented two minivans to take us to Boone. Ken once again came along to help the supervision and with the driving (sophomores, of course). We spent four nights at Appalachian State University, participating in a camp that included more than 500 runners from about 25 different schools across the southeast. The final three nights we spent in a comfortable mountain cabin named "Top Snaggy," just a couple of miles from ASU.

I've been taking my teams up to the Carolinas on trips like this since my second year of coaching cross country in 1996. That first trip was the idea of my friend, Jim Parrish, who was coaching the Jesuit team with me. Jim had moved from North Carolina back to his hometown of Tampa to spend a year caring for his elderly father who was very ill. Jim had run cross country at Jesuit and at Furman University where we were classmates. He has a master's degree in sports administration from Ohio University as well as a strong background in exercise physiology. He was far more qualified to coach cross country than I was.

Since this was during my tenure as athletic director, I hired him to coach the cross country team at Jesuit, and I became his assistant. He also took a part-time job at a YMCA and moved back in with his parents for the year. I learned more about coaching distance running in that one year working with Jim than in any other year. He introduced me to the world of exercise physiology, and we spent hours discussing the principles of training as well the art of coaching. Jim was very keen on trail running. At the time, my only running experience was on roads so my team ran almost exclusively on paved roads. Jim hated running roads and dragged me all over the greater Tampa area looking for better trails for the team (and us) to run.

"We need to take these kids on a trail running trip all over the southeast," he announced one day. That summer, Atlanta was hosting the U.S. Olympic trials, and we made that the centerpiece of our road trip. We loaded our top eight runners in a school van and proceeded to take them on a trip that would introduce them to some of our region's best trails, several college campuses and, of course, the Olympic trials.

The first leg of the trip was a nine-hour drive from Tampa to Atlanta, where we had tickets to the afternoon track session of the trials. I finally exited the interstate in Atlanta, came to a traffic light, and stopped the van. As I waited for the light to turn green, an unmarked police car pulled up beside me, and the driver motioned for me to roll my window down. The deputy was a relatively young woman with an angry look on her face. I rolled the window down and asked her what was wrong.

"I'll tell you what's wrong," she snapped. "Somebody in your van thinks it's funny to display pornography to passing cars." That was about the last thing I expected her to say. She went on for a few more seconds about how I need to teach my boys some common decency, and finally she drove off. I was livid. I was exhausted from driving nine hours and mortified by the admonishment I had just received. I pulled the van over into a parking lot, and let out one of the angriest tirades of my coaching career. Generally speaking, the boys I coach are usually very well-behaved. With teenage boys, however, there is always going to be some mischief. I've had other disappointments on these trips, but I will never forget that first one.

Another thing I learned on that first trip was that it's much easier to take your team to a camp where there are meals and activities regularly provided for them, rather than staying in random hotels, planning daily activities for the boys and eating at different restaurants every day like we did that first year. It was exhausting.

Since then, we have been going to camps associated with a college. I'm partial to the beautiful mountains of North Carolina, so we went to Brevard College for the first few years, and we've been going to Appalachian State since 2002. Even with all of the built-in resources these camps provide, looking after that many boys for seven days takes a physical and mental toll. Anything can happen. I've made no less than three trips to the emergency room at the Boone Medical Center over the years. The worst incident occurred during what should have been the most relaxing time at camp, soaking in a stream.

In 2006 (my final year as the Jesuit coach), Greg and I had taken the boys to a local swimming area that features a cold, invigorating stream. Some of our boys noticed a few local teens jumping from a platform into the cold water below. We saw several do it right in front of us, so it seemed safe. However, when Tanner, a rising junior runner, landed in the water, one of his legs hit a rock below the surface. I knew something was wrong when his head didn't go under the water. He was looking straight at me when he landed, and I still remember the haunting look in his eyes. I feared for the worst. I imagined his legs had snapped under him.

Greg and I swam out to him and helped him to the shore, while a couple of boys hustled back to the van to call 911. When we got Tanner to the shore, I was somewhat relieved to see that neither leg looked obviously broken. We quickly saw the actual wound. Something below the surface had punctured his leg in the upper shin of his left leg. The gash was nearly half-an-inch wide—and deep. You could see to the bone.

The ambulance arrived quickly, but then we had another major problem. We had climbed down a steep, rugged trail to get to the swimming area, so now we had to figure out how to lift him up and out on a stretcher. Tanner was the tallest runner on the team at about six feet, three inches. It hurt too much for him to put any weight on it, and we didn't know if there was a fracture that we couldn't see. I still don't know how we did it. When I visit that area now, I marvel at how we were ever able to get Tanner back up to the parking area. Luckily, he only required several stitches, and there was only a slight fracture. Unfortunately, though, he did not fully recover in time to compete that season.

If Tanner's injury had been more serious, I really doubt I could have even continued coaching. I was traumatized. For several days, I was unable to sleep at night without re-experiencing the frightful event. In fact, whenever it did replay in my mind, it was always much worse that the actual event. Even today, I can't recall this story without getting a sick feeling. Needless to say, Greg and I have never again allowed any of our runners to jump into those streams from any height. My runners today think I'm being silly and stubborn when they see local kids or runners from other teams jumping in and having fun, but I can hardly bear to watch those other kids doing it without seeing images of Tanner's near disaster.

Boone is only about 15 minutes from Blowing Rock, North Carolina, where we traveled four of the seven days during this year's camp to run the beautiful carriage trails at Moses Cone State Park. The signature run in that park is called "The Fire Tower Run" and starts at Bass Lake, which is about 4,000 feet above sea level and winds uphill for about 5.6 miles to an elevation of nearly 4,600 feet. Once you get to the top, you reach Flat Top Tower, a 60 foot steel lookout fire tower with steep open-air stairs leading to the top observation deck. This is the run that the older boys talk about all summer with such hype that the newcomers to camp begin to imagine something much harder than it really is (which is part of the fun).

This year, we ran to the fire tower on the first and last days of camp to enjoy breathtaking views of the Appalachian Mountains and to feel the rush of cool winds blowing over our tired, sweaty bodies. We ran every morning, alternating hilly climbs with more gentle trails along riverbanks. Each day also included a bone-chilling soak in cold mountain streams and waterfalls to help our muscles recover for the next day's effort. By the end of the week, our top three runners ran a total of 70 miles, and most of the others ran 60 miles. I was able to cover a total of 41 miles during the week, bringing my monthly total to 131 miles—one mile over my goal.

On the final morning of the ASU team camp, we participated in the 2-mile camp cross country race. Normally, I believe that summertime is for training and not racing, so in the past I have usually taken my team for a long trail run while most of the other campers participated in the two-mile cross country race. This year, however, I decided to use the race to change up the routine and get the boys a little more calloused to racing. A few of our guys suffer from race anxiety, so I wanted to balance our training with some friendly, low-key race experiences to help desensitize them to the racing environment.

It turned out to be a pretty good morale booster as our team took third place among the 19 teams that participated, and six of our 11 boys who ran earned medals for finishing in the top 30 out of about 150 participants in the boys race. I also think this race experience will be good preparation for our end-of-summer time-trial, which will take place on the first official day of practice, exactly two weeks after our return from camp. The time trial will serve as a way to choose the varsity runners for our first meet of the year, which will be the Déjà Vu Invitational on Saturday, September 9, here in Tampa.

As much experience as I have coaching cross country teams, I am still not confident trying to predict during the summer which boys will be in our top seven late in the fall for the championship meets. Some regular season meets allow you to enter up to 10 runners in a varsity race. This helps me to choose the final top seven because I get to see more of them running head-to-head. Generally, the better they do in the summer the better they do in the fall, but that's not always the case. Some kids look great in the summer and come out blazing fast in the first race or two before slowly fading to the back of the pack. Other boys frustrate me all summer by missing workouts and showing up out of shape, yet somehow manage to find their way onto the varsity squad by late fall. Genetics is a powerful thing.

This year's team has trained more and trained harder over the summer than any team I have ever coached. Our team leader and top runner this season is definitely Travis. He transferred to Plant halfway through his freshman year, and he has steadily evolved into an elite runner. Last year, as a junior, he was consistently our team's number two runner. In one race, he actually broke the school record for 5K, but finished just a couple of seconds behind our number one runner who now owns that school record. In the spring, he missed breaking our school's 3,200-meter record by less than two seconds. If he continues to progress, he will own both of those records before he graduates.

One of the biggest challenges for this year's team is finding someone to take Travis's place as a close number two runner. Our second best returning runner is definitely Curtis. He was consistently about 30 seconds behind Travis in most cross country races last season. Even though Curtis is a senior, last year was his first full year as a distance runner. He did not join our team until the spring of his sophomore year. He was one of our big surprises last year, consistently placing third on our team in his first year of cross country. Generally, a runner's greatest improvement occurs between his first and second year of training, so hopefully he can close the gap between himself and Travis.

We have another senior, John, who is in his first year of cross country. Like Curtis did last year, John might make an immediate impact. John gave up football last spring to run track. Initially, he was motivated by his girlfriend, who was a cross country and track runner. When John asked me about joining our team for training runs last January, I was hesitant at first. As much as I am always on the lookout for new distance runners, John was already in the second half of his junior year, and I was skeptical about adding someone who had so little time left to develop as a runner. I also wondered if he just wanted to hang out near his girlfriend.

In a very short time, it became obvious that John is a natural distance runner. Within a few weeks, he was staying up with our varsity runners in training, and when the track season started, he was racing right with the middle of our varsity pack after just over one month of training. As I could have predicted based on his lack of sufficient preparation, he peaked in mid-season and started experiencing pain in his shins.

He also became distracted and lost focus on distance running for a while. One weekend I drove by our school's football field and saw him playing Ultimate Frisbee with some friends. The problem was that I had given him a couple of days off from running to recover from shin pain, and there he was sprinting and leaping all over the field. By the time we started our summer training, however, John was "all in" once again, and he has been ever since. In the camp race, he finished third on our team.

Two other seniors, Jacob and Sam, have experience running in our top seven, and both ran close to 17:00 for 5K last year. A sixth senior, Joe, transferred from Greensboro, North Carolina, last fall and worked his way up to the front of our junior varsity team by the season's end. We call him "Crazy Joe" because he has a great finishing kick at the end of races that is generally accompanied by a primal yell that he blasts into the air as he passes runners before crossing the finish line. The rule of thumb is, if you can hear Joe coming, he's gonna get you!

Though it seems as if our team is going to be dominated by seniors, there will likely be at least a couple of underclassmen in our top seven. Last year's most improved runner, Bryce, is a junior who had the best track season of any of his classmates. He finished the spring season by running 16:42 for 5K in a local road race. Two other juniors, Anatoly and Jason, were actually ahead of Bryce last fall, and seem poised for their breakthroughs.

There are two sophomores, Carlos and Josh, who went with us to camp. Carlos had a very good freshman cross country season, and then a stellar rookie track season, winning the freshman mile race at one of the largest track meets of the year in a time of 4:46. Josh also broke five minutes for the mile during his freshman track season, which shows that he has natural talent. Josh is the son of our legendary girls' cross country coach, Roy Harrison. Roy has earned more state titles for a single gender than any coach in Florida history. It's a little nerve-racking having such a successful coach watching me train his son, but he's been a great resource and sounding board for me.

Finally, there's Matt, a freshman runner who went to camp with us, and who just might squeeze his way into the varsity mix. Matt has never run cross country before, but he has competed nationally in track, mostly racing in the 800 meters. Matt was also a standout youth league football player who played on an all-star team that traveled to Texas to compete against the best middle school football players in the country. Coach Weiner, our head football coach, has known about Matt for three years and was expecting him to play football this fall. Instead, Matt made a decision last winter to give up football and go out for cross country at Plant to focus on his career as a prep runner. He actually chose cross country over football!

It was a risk for me to take a freshman on our trip to camp for many reasons, but I wanted him to meet our top guys right away and confirm to him that he made the right choice. So far, he has progressed beyond my expectations, and he has seamlessly blended into our varsity training group. Matt's story could be one of the most interesting subplots of this season.

Though I can't predict which seven of those 12 boys are going to be the ones to toe the line at the State Meet in November, this is what we have to work with. Barring some last minute unexpected transfer from another school, this is it. Is it enough to win our school's first boys' cross country state title? Time will tell. I know for sure that I'm luckier than most coaches. Any one of those 12 would be a top-seven runner at any other school in our county and just about any school in the state. Each one of them made a serious commitment this summer to raise their level of fitness, and it's starting to show.

Likewise, time will tell regarding my own training. July went just about exactly as planned. Before I left for camp, I did two consecutive 40-mile weeks, followed by a week at the beach where I only ran three times for a total of 10 miles. The 40-mile weeks were not much of a struggle, as I ran most of it during team training. My legs are still holding up well, and the increase in mileage has been gradual enough that my body seems to be adapting quite well. This month's goal is 145 miles, which will only require me to run about 35 miles per week, so I am confident I can keep the progression going.

During the cross country camp, I "accidentally" did an awesome long run of 13 miles. The day after the camp race, we drove the boys to Damascus, Virginia, where we hopped on the Virginia Creeper Trail, a converted railroad passage characterized by smooth, gently rolling surfaces with numerous wooden bridges crossing over crystal clear streams. I intended the run to be 11 miles, and I used my trail map to indicate where we should turn around to get the right distance. According to my map, it should have been about 5.5 miles of gradual incline from my starting place to a 100-foot high, 500-feet long trestle bridge. Apparently, my trail map was faulty because it took me all of an hour to reach that bridge.

Since I had given myself a significant head start on the boys, I reached the turnaround mark a few minutes before they did, and I couldn't warn them about my mistake until they also had gone out way too far. When I headed back and eventually passed the boys going the opposite way, they quickly let me know that it was much farther than I figured. Because I had given myself a three-mile head start after I dropped the boys off on the trail, their "accidental" distance turned out to be about 16 miles by the time we all made it back to the van. Oops. At least there was a wonderfully refreshing stream to soak in when we were done. Aaaaahhhh . . .

The fact that I did a 13-mile(ish) run already in July is promising since that was my goal for my August long runs, and I have already done it once successfully. Of course, the weather was nearly 20 degrees cooler and the humidity several points lower on the Virginia Creeper than it will be in Temple Terrace for my next Sunday morning long run, but at least I know I can cover that distance without any significant problems. I am actually looking forward to getting back to those Sunday morning Temple Terrace runs with Greg. He and his team were also at camp, and he seemed to be running relatively pain-free though he is still struggling with some leg and foot issues.

One more thing happened at camp. I started having daydreams about retiring from coaching. The farther we got into the week and the more tired my mind and body became, the more I felt myself imagining what my life might be like after I stop coaching cross country and track. When I mentioned this to Linda, she did not seem surprised. I even got the sense that perhaps she's even hopeful I might have more time to spend with her in the next few years. As proud as I am of all that I have accomplished in coaching, I do have regrets about some of the sacrifices I have chosen to make.

I know that my obsession with being with the boys throughout the summer and fall has caused Linda to miss certain opportunities that would have included me. Our friends, Dennis and Caroline Jones, for example, have been trying to get us to vacation in Aspen with them every September for the past few years. September is Linda's birthday month, and I regret that I have never sacrificed my sacred season time to accept this generous offer and celebrate her birthday in such a beautiful location. My reasoning is always the same. If I would not allow any of my runners to leave for vacation during the season, how can I?

It's not that Linda and I have not had our share of vacations and treasured experiences. We have traveled all over Europe, vacationed in Hawaii and visited several of the big cities and attractions around the United States. It's just that I know there have been times when Linda, and I am sure my children too, have been shortchanged.

I've had thoughts of retiring from coaching before, and I have always found the motivation to start all over again once the season was over. But every year it seems to get a little harder to summon up the will and stamina to keep myself and three dozen or so boys focused and committed. I don't think I would be happy doing it with less effort and commitment. I have coaching friends whose teams are fairly competitive and who put far less time and energy into it than I do. A small part of me even envies their ability to do that and be happy with whatever success their teams might achieve. I just don't see that as an option for me. I have always coached every season with everything I have as if it were my last. Could this be the year that it really is?

The 2011 Plant Boys Cross Country team enjoys a cold soak in a
stream near Boone, NC.
(Photo courtesy of Ken Mersereau)

Chapter Eight
SWEET TEA AND JESUS

August 2011

August is behind me now, and I ran 148 miles, which was three more than my goal. The funny thing is I spent most of August thinking I was supposed to run 160 miles. Somehow, I got the number 160 in my head, and it got stuck there until August was nearly over. If I had gone back and read my own journal, I would have realized I only needed to run 145 miles. It was frustrating because it started to make me doubt I could reach my mileage goal. By the third week, I had resolved that I was just too busy and tired to squeeze in enough running to get the mileage I thought I needed. During the final week of August, it finally dawned on me that I had made a mistake. By that time, I was easily on pace for my actual goal, and I was even able to give myself an extra day off.

That experience makes me question whether I can meet my monthly mileage progression goals. I started back to school in the middle of August, and my time to rest and recover from runs has all but disappeared. Is 160 miles just too much for me to run in one month, or was it just too big of a jump from the 130-mile total of the previous month? I originally intended to gradually increase my monthly total to 200 miles by the end of the year. That seems quite unrealistic now. I am definitely going to find out soon if I can handle 160 miles in a month because that is my goal for September—for real this time.

On the other hand, my weekly long runs went very well in August. I did a 13-mile run with Greg every Sunday. Each long run went just a little better than the previous one. We did three of the four long runs on the hilly Temple Terrace course. The fourth and final one we did from my house, out along the Bayshore, around the Davis Islands neighborhood and back. We also got lucky with the weather. During the last two Sunday long runs, there were plenty of clouds to protect us from the rising sun. It was still warm and muggy, but doing long runs in Tampa under cloudless skies after sunrise is a recipe for disaster.

School has also started for my cross country team, and they are also struggling with the transition to waking up early for school, grinding through the school day, completing homework and then training at a high level in the August heat. We have gradually switched gears in our training runs to include some faster running. Most of our miles are still run at an aerobic pace of about 7:00-7:30 per mile, but about twice a week we are doing faster tempo runs.

Before the boys returned to school we did a 2-mile time trial on August 15, the first official day of practice. The boys were motivated by a couple of goals. First, I made it known that the top 10 finishers in the time trial would be running the varsity race in our first meet of the season. Also, any runner who broke 11:00 for the 2-mile race would get his own warm-up jacket with the team logo on the front and his name on the back.

I was really hoping for even the slightest break in the hot, humid weather so we could see some fast times, but that wasn't to be the case. Not only did it seem slightly hotter and muggier than usual when we arrived at Al Lopez Park for our time trial, it started pouring rain about halfway into the race. I set up our digital clock at the finish line to make it seem more like a real race, and a few parents even showed up for this Monday morning extravaganza to see their boys perform. By the time Travis started his final kick to the finish, it was raining so hard that we could barely see him coming from 50 meters away. The times were not as fast as we had hoped, but the results were still promising. The top 10 finishers included:

Travis	9:57
Curtis	10:14
John	10:25
Sam	10:27
Jacob	10:29
Bryce	10:34
Anatoly	10:38
Matt	10:48
Joe	10:51
Carlos	10:57

The top five finishers were all seniors. This was about what I expected. One of the drawbacks of having a senior-heavy team is that underclassmen don't get the opportunity to gain experience being counted on to score for the team. It will be important for next year's team that someone has experience as a top five runner. Carlos and Bryce seem to be the strongest candidates to fill that role. Carlos has strong leadership skills, so if he can make his way into the top five he can become a natural leader for the next two years. The other two underclassmen to make the top 10 list were Anatoly, who is a junior, and Matt, the freshman. Matt breaking 11:00 and making the top 10 was a pleasant surprise as well as a wake-up call for some sophomores and juniors who figured they would be in the hunt for a varsity spot.

Lawson, also a junior, broke 11:00 as well, giving us 11 runners to break that important mark. Lawson spent most of the summer training on his own while on a youth trip to Israel. Obviously, I was disappointed when I found out he would not be training with us for the summer. I did not expect that he would be able to keep up his training on his own as well as he did. He sent me weekly email reports from Israel about his training, and I was very impressed with his dedication to his running goals in challenging circumstances.

The second half of August was characterized by adjusting to the start of school. Just like my own training, the boys had become accustomed to a routine of building the whole day around that day's work out. Waking up early for school, staying up late working on assignments and keeping up with social expectations all make our high level training harder than it already is. The biggest challenge is the lack of sufficient recovery after workouts. Summer training for many runners is often characterized by sleeping in on afternoon training days and post-run naps after morning runs. It can take well into September before their bodies adjust to training through their school schedules.

One of the biggest changes I've made this year to help me with my own struggles to manage all of the practices while teaching and directing the social studies department at Plant is adding two volunteer coaches to our program. Jordan Pelaez graduated recently from the University of South Florida. During his high school days, he was a standout 800-meter runner for Middleton High School. I have known him since his middle school days when he started attending a summer running camp that I used to offer at Al Lopez

Park. I was so impressed with him that I eventually hired him to help me with the camp as a junior coach. Bryan Garcia was one of our main competitors when he was a cross country and track star at Robinson High School. He is currently a sophomore at the University of Tampa, where he runs cross country on a partial scholarship. Jordan and Bryan are incredibly positive people and have been great role models for our runners. They have given me the opportunity to delegate many of the practice duties and even entire practice sessions whenever I have had major conflicts.

Meanwhile, my marathon training plan has become a bit more complicated by the fact that Linda has been trying to convince me to attend church with her, which conflicts with my plan of doing long runs with Greg on Sunday mornings. The church service that we like to attend starts at 9:30 a.m. There is a traditional service that starts at the "traditional" time of 11:00 a.m., but it is too dull for us. Our preferred service has upbeat contemporary music, plenty of familiar faces with whom we feel connected, and best of all, serves coffee and bagels you may eat during the service.

For the most part, Linda is very supportive of my mission to get back into marathon shape. She has always been very tolerant of the sacrifices of time and energy I put into training and coaching, and she often looks for ways to help out at meets and offer support whenever I am competing. But church is important to Linda, and it's also important to her that it be important to me.

I don't mind church, and sometimes I even like church, but Sunday mornings are the only time I can do my long runs with Greg. Saturdays are taken up by coaching. I also enjoy stopping for coffee with Greg after our long runs. I don't want to have to rush home to get ready for church. The bottom line is that I enjoy my Sunday running routine more than attending church. Thank goodness I don't subscribe to a faith in which my salvation depends on regular church attendance.

My religious beliefs have evolved significantly over time, and they no longer seem to fit into any traditional belief system that I know of. My earliest religious memories relate to my grandmother, Abuela Mimi. Mimi was my mother's mother, and she lived with us briefly before passing on. During the time she stayed with us,

I remember hearing her talk about some of her Catholic beliefs. She spoke very little English. I could understand most of what she was saying when she was speaking Spanish, but I'm not sure I was always getting the full meaning. The gist of it, as I recall, had to do with eating Jesus's body and drinking his blood. Needless to say, this was very disturbing to me as a young boy with no religious background.

Eventually my parents moved me from public school to a Catholic parochial school for sixth grade. It was at St. Joseph's Catholic School that the sisters of St. Francis of Assisi started teaching me about Catholicism. I went through the First Communion training with a bunch of first-graders, which is when most Catholic school children get their training. The one bit of information I wish the good sisters had given me was to talk softly when I was in the confessional. The first time I went to confession with my class, we all lined up in alphabetical order to go into the confessional in which you can see the screened image of a priest sitting on the other side of a thin wall.

I nervously recited the words I was taught, "Bless me Father for I have sinned, this is my first confession." Then I proceeded to spill my guts about every embarrassing detail I thought might have offended Jesus. When I was done, the priest advised me to say a certain number of Catholic prayers. When I opened the door and exited the little closet, my classmates were unable to hold back their laughter. It wouldn't get much better for the next three years.

Some Catholic parochial schools offer a superior education. This one did not. The public schools that I attended prior to my middle school years at St. Joseph's School were better learning environments. The classes at St. Joseph's were more crowded than the ones I had been in, and my teachers were less effective. Two of the three years I was there, I had nuns as my teachers. I remember one of them warning me about going to high school, where I might be told lies about how men were created.

"Some scientists dug up monkey bones," she taught us, "and made the mistake of thinking that those were our ancestors' bones." At the time, this seemed perfectly plausible to me since my teacher, Sister Antoinette, looked like a monkey herself.

Jesuit High School would be my salvation from this outdated form of Catholicism. It would also be my salvation from a group of kids who never really accepted me. At St. Joseph's I arrived after all the groups of friends had been well established. I knew very little about Jesuit except that my dad wanted me to go there, and all of the other kids in my eighth-grade class at St. Joseph's, except one, were going to the rival Catholic high school. I also heard it was going to be more difficult, which suited me fine even though my eighth-grade teacher, Sister Barbara, had warned me that I "would never make it at Jesuit." Little did she know that nothing else can motivate me more than being told I "can't" do something.

The priests at Jesuit were far more intellectual and progressive than the nuns at St. Joe's. I liked most of them right away. I also finally felt like I fit in with my peers. I made more friends in my first year at Jesuit than in all three years at St. Joe's. I struggled academically during that first year as Sister Barbara predicted I would. In hindsight, especially now that I am a teacher, I realize how poorly prepared I was when I arrived at high school. By my sophomore year, I was finding success as a varsity football player, and I was also starting to find success in the classroom (after my afternoon encounter with Ms. Connors, that is). I became a leader among my peers. I felt like a big man on campus. It was a complete change from my middle school experience.

While I was at St. Joe's, I was obligated to attend mass there every Sunday. Once I got to Jesuit, I was happily liberated from that burden. Instead, I would attend mandatory mass in the Jesuit chapel during school hours once a month. Other than that, no one was pushing me to go to church on Sundays, so I stopped attending, even though my younger brother and sister were still being dragged to St. Joseph's each Sunday. Church at Jesuit was a very different experience. The priests won me over with their impressive use of reason and their emphasis on the brotherhood of our student body. They were training us as "men for others" who would be the future leaders of our society. They were also training us to think.

I started volunteering to help at mass by doing the Scripture readings. I loved the feeling of standing at the lectern in front of all of my classmates and reading the holy words. I never had any thoughts of becoming a priest, however. Like most teenagers, the thought of spending my adult life in a state of celibacy was unthinkable. But I did enjoy the time I spent in the Jesuit chapel. My Jesuit experience, as much as anything else, saved me from the worst effects of my family's dysfunction. I needed something strong and stable to keep me from being swept into the storm raging in my home, and Jesuit was the rock I could hold onto.

So I left for Furman University as a nominal Catholic, and I wandered into the world of sweet tea and Jesus. In all my Catholic school training, no one prepared me to hear the message of salvation as preached in the Bible Belt of South Carolina. When I started falling in love with Linda during my freshman year, I was wide open to the prospects of "inviting Jesus into my heart," as evangelicals like to call becoming a Christian. I sometimes joke that I would have joined just about any church if it would help me get Linda to go out with me. Linda was raised in a Southern Baptist church that preached salvation through the acceptance of Jesus as your savior. I found nothing objectionable about Jesus. Heck, I already loved Jesus. Better yet, these services were a lot livelier than I was used to. With the exception of the sermon time, which I found way too long, Baptist church seemed like more fun.

Linda and I are both born leaders, and it wasn't long before both of us found ourselves in gradually increasing roles of leadership in the church. Linda went to Furman with the idea of going into the ministry, and I soon started to share that vision. Eventually, we took jobs as co-ministers of youth at Sans Souci Baptist Church. I also found my way up to the lectern as I had at Jesuit, except this time I was able to see myself leading a congregation one day—something that had never crossed my mind in high school.

I put myself completely into this religious experience the same way I do most everything else I commit to. I studied the Bible diligently, and I adopted the traditional Baptist doctrines, including salvation by faith in Jesus alone. I started looking for more and more opportunities to preach the Word as I understood it at the time, and I always ended my sermons with the traditional Baptist altar call inviting sinners to come, repent and accept Jesus as savior and Lord.

What is most scary to me now as I look back on this period is that I had an answer for everything. I was the exact kind of ideologue that now annoys me the most. In my reckless abandon to be the best at whatever I was doing, I let my passion subdue my reason. I knew I was right about what I believed because my faith and my own personal experience proved it so to me.

Linda and I were all set to head off to a Baptist seminary in San Francisco after graduating from Furman. Then I got cold feet. My mother's life was spiraling downward since her divorce from my father during my freshman year of college. My mom attempted suicide more than once when I was growing up, and threatened suicide more often than I want to remember. My gut feeling was that her suicidal tendencies were growing stronger, and I felt that somehow I could help if I moved back to Tampa to look out for her. I also couldn't bear the thought of her dying while I was on the other side of the country, unable to stop her from hurting herself. I've always regretted not taking Linda to San Francisco like we planned.

Linda and I both took jobs in Tampa as teachers. Teaching was temporary until I was ready to finally get to seminary and prepare for life as a Baptist minister. I got several opportunities to preach at Seminole Heights Baptist Church in Tampa, where Linda and I took jobs as part-time co-ministers of youth. The pastor, Dr. Pinner, was a skilled preacher who was more intellectual and progressive than most of the Baptist preachers I met in South Carolina. He mentored me by encouraging me to read some of the classic authors of Christian literature, like Dietrich Bonhoeffer and C.S. Lewis. I was impressed by the way Dr. Pinner incorporated reason, logic and intellect into his messages. His guidance led me to look more closely at my own message, and grow more open to the various experiences of others.

After three years in Tampa, we finally made the decision to move to Wake Forest, North Carolina, for me to attend Southeastern Baptist Seminary. In hindsight, this was one of the most selfish and impulsive decisions I have ever made. Our daughter Melody had just turned one year old when I decided we were all leaving our home in Tampa so I could start seminary in August. The decision to go to seminary in North Carolina rather than California, as we originally planned, was mainly because we wanted to keep our first child as close to her grandparents as possible. Southeastern is only 90 minutes from Winston-Salem, where Linda's family lives.

79

We rented a two-room duplex 15 minutes from campus, and I took a job as a part-time assistant pastor at a Baptist church about 30 minutes away. After several failed attempts to find a babysitter, we finally got someone to watch Melody, and Linda took a teaching job at a private school on the Duke University campus, which was also a 30-minute commute from our duplex.

I started classes in the fall of 1984, and by Thanksgiving I realized that seminary was not for me. We stayed in North Carolina through the next spring. Linda finished the school year teaching at the private school, and I continued to work as an assistant pastor. I also took jobs as a substitute teacher and a bus driver, and I took a paper route to earn extra money. I even managed to earn some graduate credits at the nearby University of North Carolina Central, which enabled me to obtain my Florida teaching certificate when we returned.

I am at a loss to explain how and why seminary just didn't work out. Not since St. Joseph's had I felt so out of place in a school. Bad timing was partly to blame. Even during my most conservative evangelical period, I was still relatively open-minded. My religion teachers at Furman had mostly been fairly liberal, at least by Southern Baptist standards. Just as I was enrolling at Southeastern, several professors were let go for failing to sign a pledge acknowledging their belief in the "inerrancy of Scripture." This meant they had to agree to a literal interpretation of the entire Bible to keep their jobs. They refused and were fired. I wasn't educated enough to prove either side right or wrong, but I instinctively knew that firing those professors was not right.

I wish I could say that it was this theological dissonance which drove me away from seminary, but it's probably more accurate to say that I quit because I just didn't think that the ministry would ever be as much fun as teaching and coaching. I went there because I thought I was "called" to preach the Christian gospel. It was an honest mistake, and I learned something about myself. I only wish I had not uprooted my wife and our one-year-old baby daughter to do it. When we got back to Tampa, we were lucky that we were able to move right back into our house which we had been renting out for the past year, and I was able to get the job teaching and coaching football at a Middleton Junior High.

Seminole Heights Baptist hired a new youth director after we left, but Linda and I returned to that church. Money was tighter than ever after incurring so many moving expenses, so I was working four different jobs for a couple of years after returning. Not only was I teaching and coaching at the inner-city public middle school, but I also worked three night shifts per week at one funeral home, and I was doing lawn care once a week at another funeral home. It was during an otherwise ordinary night shift when I had one of the most profound religious awakenings of my life.

My main duty during the night shift, which was from 10 p.m. to 6 a.m., was answering phones for several different funeral homes, which were all owned by the same company that bought my dad's business when he retired. If I got a call from a family or a hospital, I would answer the phone with the name of the funeral home that corresponded with the blinking light on the phone. Occasionally, I would get the name wrong and totally confuse the caller. Sometimes, callers who were shopping around for a funeral home would be surprised to hear the same voice answer the phone each time they called a "different" funeral home.

For the most part, I could usually sleep through the night with minimal interruptions. Usually, I would watch some TV until I could fall asleep. One night, I stumbled across an old black and white movie called *Inherit the Wind* with Spencer Tracy and Gene Kelly. The movie was made in 1960, and it is based on the true story of the Scope's "Monkey Trial" of 1925, in which a biology teacher is on trial for breaking a state law which prohibited the teaching of evolution in public schools.

The trial featured two of America's greatest legal minds, Clarence Darrow for the defense and William Jennings Bryan for the prosecution. Somehow, in that cramped funeral home bedroom on that small TV with rabbit-ear antennas, I was mesmerized by the dialogue. The prosecution wanted to put evolution on trial, but instead it was the defense who put the Bible on trial. When Bryan boldly takes the stand to defend his literal interpretation of Scripture, Darrow methodically exposes the Bible's numerous factual errors and inconsistencies. In the end, it is clear that Darrow's intent was not to discredit the Bible as much as to protect every man's right to read it and decide for himself what it means. He was defending our right to think.

"An idea is a greater monument than a cathedral. And the advance of man's knowledge is a greater miracle than all the sticks turned to snakes or the parting of the waters," the counsel for the defense argued passionately.

In one scene of the movie, it is revealed that the biology teacher left the church after the preacher suggested in a sermon that a little boy who drowned was going to be denied eternal life in heaven because his parents never had him baptized. I immediately recognized the grotesque nature of such a doctrine. Yet, I had preached similar messages myself regarding the "narrow path" that leads to heaven. Never again could I dare believe, much less preach to others, that professing Jesus as one's savior is the only path to heaven. What kind of god would let someone's answer to a question determine their eternal fate? No god I wanted to believe in—I knew that for certain.

It wasn't long after this religious revelation that my mother finally escaped the pain she knew in this world. According to my old faith, she would suffer the same fate as the unbaptized little boy in the movie. I knew that could not be the case. For all of my mother's faults and demons, she was one of the most loving people on earth. She suffered abuse from an alcoholic father and battled all of her life with depression and alcoholism. Drinking was her surest form of relief, and it was also the poison that slowly killed her. By the time I delivered the eulogy at her funeral, there was not a shred of doubt in my mind that any god who might exist would readily greet her and give her the peaceful rest she deserved.

Chapter Nine

THE BEAR

September 2011

September was a reality check for the monthly mileage goals of my marathon training plan. I only managed to log 114 of the 160 miles I had planned to run. I was afraid this would eventually happen once the competitive cross country season started and the priority of my energy and focus shifted to my team. On a positive note, the long runs have continued to progress on schedule. Though my legs are nearly always sore, I have avoided even minor injuries that might result in a loss of training.

Greg and I changed our Sunday long run strategy this month by alternating 15-mile runs from my house along the Bayshore/ Davis Islands route with 10 to 12-mile hilly runs in Temple Terrace. We repeated a two-mile loop on the hilliest section of the Temple Terrace course three to four times during each of those runs. Repeating hilly loops is a strategy that Greg has used successfully in the past to prepare for many marathon courses, especially Boston's famous "Heartbreak Hill." Alternating the venues and the theme of the Sunday runs has helped alleviate the tedium that can accompany marathon training.

Another positive note regarding September is that my team is progressing nearly as well as I could have hoped back in June when we started preparing for this season. In our first meet of the season, we finished fifth place in the elite division of the Déjà Vu Invitational here in Tampa. It was a good start to the season. The two teams from our 4-A classification that we knew we would be chasing this year, Miami Columbus and Orlando Colonial, both beat us.

As I described it to one reporter, "It was as good as we expected, but not as good as we hoped for." Part of me was hoping that we would emerge from this meet much closer to the top two teams in our class than we did. Colonial's team time was 29 seconds per man faster than ours, and the Columbus team time was 17 seconds per man better than our boys.

Mike Boza

The race was three miles rather than the normal 5K (3.1 miles). This was a decision I made as the meet director, primarily to re-live the course length when the state meet was first held at this course back in 2002 (hence, the meet's name, Déjà Vu). But the very wet, muddy conditions made the times a bit slower than usual 5K times even though we ran a shorter course. Our top 5 runners were:

Travis	5th	16:26
Curtis	19th	16:53
John	29th	17:15
Carlos	36th	17:29
Sam	39th	17:30
Top 5 Average		*17:07*

We convincingly defeated every other team from our classification besides Columbus and Colonial. The other two teams that beat us were the top two teams from the 3-A classification. One of those teams, Estero, only beat us by a slim margin. The other 3-A school, Belen Jesuit, won the meet by a large margin, and it looks like they will emerge as the dominant Florida team in any class this season. In all honesty, if Belen was in 4-A this year, we would have almost no chance to win the state meet. At least we have a fighting chance to catch Colonial and Columbus, even if they both got the best of us to start the season.

Plant was the host school, and I was the meet director for this season-opening meet that featured 77 teams and 1,188 runners from across the state. I'm not sure why I invest so much of my time and energy into hosting these big-time meets. Early in my cross country coaching career, I considered it an important step in the emergence of our program at Jesuit. I believed that getting our name on a major meet and getting the best competition in the state to come run against us in our home town was an important ingredient of becoming a championship program.

When it comes to planning and running these mega-meets, I'm pretty good at it, but it does not come easily for me or without some real costs. As the meet approaches, the stress builds. Once the meet starts, so does the constant stream of problems and concerns, mostly from other coaches who have never even tried to host a major meet. The cost comes mostly in my inability to spend the time I need with my athletes before and after the race to help them get the most out of the experience.

When I put on this meet last year, the event was marred by several under-trained, overheated runners who collapsed and required medical attention. Even though I had hired two trainers to be on hand, several parents took it upon themselves to call 911 even though most were just overcome by running too hard in the heat and humidity without proper preparation. One mom pleaded with one of our trainers to tell her what was wrong with her daughter.

"I don't understand it," she pleaded nervously. "My daughter says she's never felt like this before."

"Is this her first race?" The trainer asked.

"Why, yes it is" the mom replied.

"Well, this is what it feels like when you race your first 5K." Duh . . .

By the halfway point of the 2010 meet, we had four different ambulances respond to various 911 calls, none of which was serious. At one point, a fire and rescue department chief sought me out and gave me an angry lecture about making unnecessary 911 calls. It was hard to explain to him that we had no control over the people making those calls.

In addition to the hot, humid conditions, the course was saturated with water from several days of downpours, and the runners were forced to slosh through several deep puddles of muddy water. Several runners lost their shoes as they literally got sucked off of their feet when they tried to lift them out of the mud. The following day when I went back to pick up the equipment left there from the night before, there were still some shoes that had been left in the mud. I was resolved that I would never put this meet on again.

Somehow, sometime after the worst memories of that meet had waned, I decided to give it one more try this season. This time I hired an EMT crew to be conspicuously on site near the finish line, and I limited the number of teams. The day before the meet, it appeared that the mud would not be nearly as bad as last year. After we finished setting up the course on race day, however, a large thunderstorm with heavy wind and rain came through and, within a couple of hours, left the course even more flooded than the previous year.

With slightly lower temps and fewer teams this year, the number of runners "falling out" was significantly minimized. There was one serious moment when a local runner collapsed from dehydration and had to be taken into the ambulance to get intravenous fluids. After a brief period in the ambulance, the EMT crew decided to transport him to the hospital, and they called another crew to take their place. As they started to drive away from the finish line area, the driver chose to take a route through the grass rather than the sidewalk on which they entered.

When the ambulance started to climb a small, grassy hill, the back wheels started to spin in the wet, muddy grass, and eventually the vehicle was hopelessly stuck. The second ambulance eventually came and transported the stricken runner, who was fine by the time he reached the hospital. It was well after 11p.m., however, before a wrecker finally arrived to tow the ambulance out of the mud.

Needless to say, putting on this meet on the second weekend of September was the primary reason that I started to fall so far behind in my mileage goal. For the next week after the meet I was still suffering from the physical and mental fatigue of staging the meet, while keeping up with my teaching and coaching duties. I called a coach friend who I thought might be interested in putting on this meet in the future as a fundraiser for his relatively new program. He's thinking about it. In the meantime, I'm done putting on mega-meets. And I really, really mean it this time. Really.

Two weeks prior to our first meet, we had an epic practice to help get us ready to race. The workout is called "The Bear." There are many variations of "The Bear" and it can be adapted to various abilities, but the classic "Papa Bear" consists of four miles in 26 minutes (6:30/mile) followed by three miles in 18 minutes (6:00/mile), then two miles in 11 minutes and finally one mile in 5 minutes or less. It's a total of ten miles run at progressively faster paces. The recovery between these bouts of paced running consists of five minutes of light jogging. The creator of this monster workout is the legendary Brent Haley, whose teams at Largo High won a state record of 10 state championships in the 1970s and 1980s.

Our team has tried various adaptations of the Bear, but none of our runners had ever conquered the full "Papa Bear." Travis started pleading with me over the summer to give him a chance to

In retrospect, it was a very good idea to travel to Tallahassee for this meet. The other major meet we considered going to on that weekend was the University of Florida meet. The only advantage I saw regarding that meet was the shorter distance we would have to travel. Gainesville is only two hours away. Since this was going to be our lone overnight trip for the season, I did not mind the extra driving time. The University of Florida meet ended up being a horrible experience for several teams. The meet director allowed nearly 70 teams to enter the same race. The boy's race had to be re-started four times because runners were being pushed to the ground by the stampede of over 400 runners.

As a result of the overcrowded conditions, plus the same heat wave that slowed our race down, the times from the University of Florida race were slower than expected. Our two main rivals in 4-A, Colonial and Columbus, took second and third in that meet, with team times that were slower than what we ran in Tallahassee. Belen Jesuit won again, as they had done at Déjà Vu.

Whenever you compare results of teams that compete in different races, you run into a seemingly unending list of opinions about how the two different venues compared to one another. Some people obsess over what these numbers mean and analyze the results using several types of statistical analyses. Sometimes I get sucked into that sort of obsession, but generally I go with my intuition. My gut told me that, though we may not already be better than those two teams as the times indicated, we had closed the gap. We will have to wait until we all meet again at the Pre-State Meet in mid-October to really find out where we stand.

One thing is for sure. I feel more confident about my team's training than my own preparation for the marathon. It's time to get my own running back in order. I need to find the time and energy to log the miles necessary to make my goal of another sub 4-hour marathon. It's clear to me now I will not be able to achieve goal of increasing my total miles every month to a total of 200 miles per month. At the very least, I would like to maintain the monthly mileage I reached in August when I ran 148 miles. I plan to try log at least 150 miles each of the next three months. That means averaging just over 35 miles a week.

I do plan to keep up my weekly long run mileage progression and eventually reach 21 miles for my longest run in December. On the weeks when I do my longer runs with Greg, I can get 50 percent or more of my weekly miles in a single Sunday run. This will give me a chance to recover from those long runs without stressing over the mileage lost by taking a couple of days off from running. As long as I can keep increasing the distance of my long run, I will be doing the most important part of the marathon preparation.

It has gotten easier for me to run with our JV boys at some of our practices. The rookie runners on our team have now progressed to the point where they can all do at least six miles at a reasonable pace during our easy running days on the Bayshore. This makes it easier for me to get some mileage done without having to nurse along some out-of-shape runner who can't hold the pace. On a recent easy run day on Bayshore, I decided to take the freshman group on a little adventure.

I had told them they were going to do a 6-mile run, so they assumed that they would run the usual route of going two miles along Bayshore Boulevard and then crossing the Davis Island bridge. There is a water fountain at a marina on the island that is about three miles from our starting point. They usually run to that fountain, get a quick drink, head back to the Bayshore and then back to our starting spot.

On this hot Thursday afternoon, I had a surprise for them. Instead of making the right turn onto the Davis Island bridge, we went straight across the Platt Street bridge that goes into downtown Tampa. Once in the downtown area, they all followed closely behind me as I made a left turn down Ashley Street. I could sense the excitement, and I could hear some of them trying to figure out where we were going. Tampa's downtown is mostly a business district, and only a few of the kids have probably spent much time there. Even those who have been downtown had never run on those streets before, so my goal of surprising them with something completely different was working. And then it got better.

I took them along a sidewalk that eventually took us to a riverfront city park. Near the entrance to the park there is a water play area where jets under the sidewalk send up tall streams of water. As we approached the park, I picked up my speed and started heading right towards the fountains. I could hear some of the kids behind me wondering if I was really going to do it. Seconds later, I was bursting through walls of water for about 30 meters as the boys followed right behind me trying their best to keep the forceful jets of water from going up their noses and into their eyes. We came out soaking wet on the other side and stood around for a few minutes laughing and enjoying the cool break from the hot, sticky afternoon before starting our jog back.

I wish all of my runs with the freshmen were as lighthearted and fun as that jog to the water fountains. On a subsequent run, I found myself slowly gaining on the freshmen group as they made their way down Bayshore. By the time I was within earshot of the main pack of freshmen, only one of the boys was aware I was around. As I tuned in to hear what they were saying, I overheard them telling very inappropriate jokes. I was furious. On days like that my job as a coach becomes very challenging.

I thought long and hard about how to handle this issue. I have learned to take my time with situations like these. In the past, I was more likely to immediately start blasting away at the culprits. I still explode occasionally, though I've become less prone to do so over the years. I often regret my "explosions" and have to later apologize for letting my righteous passion carry me too far. Losing my cool often results in losing the ability to have a genuine teaching moment. After several years of coaching at Jesuit, I found out that, because of this tendency, some of the boys secretly referred to me as "The Thriller" (from the classic Michael Jackson video when he transforms into a monster).

This time I sternly told the boys that I was very angry and disappointed. Then I told them we would certainly address the issue before practice the next day. I'm sure most of them wished I had just gotten it over with right then. Instead, I let them go home and wonder what fate awaited them. At the next practice, I called aside the group that had made the distasteful jokes and gave them a passionate, yet calculated, "thrilling." I decided on a combination of teaching and threatening to make the boys understand the kind of behavior I expect of them. I'm pretty sure most of them will remember that talk for a good while. Why can't every practice be a fountain run?

I soon had to turn my attention back to our top varsity runners as we traveled to Titusville on the final day of September to compete in the flrunners.com Invitational in Titusville. It's one of the largest and most competitive meets in the southeastern United States. Rather than entering our varsity team in the Saturday morning elite race as I normally would, I entered them in the Friday afternoon "large-school" race. Part of my reasoning for racing the less-competitive Friday race was that the first weekend of October was also the date of this fall's first SAT test, and I did not want to force any of our seniors to choose between racing and testing. The last thing I want is a parent blaming me for poor SAT scores because their son could not take the test on his first choice of dates. As it turned out, two of our seniors ended up taking the SAT that morning.

We left school at midday on Friday and went out for lunch. We took our time driving to Titusville, but we still arrived about two hours early. At first, it looked like it might be rainy or overcast, but by race time the sun had returned. Once again, we raced in warm, muggy conditions. Our team dominated the field as we had expected, taking five of the top 12 places in the race of over 220 runners. Travis took the lead just before the midway point of the race and went on to win easily in 16:10. Curtis had a breakthrough race. He passed four runners in the final mile to take second place in 16:26. Our top five included:

Travis	1st	16:10
Curtis	2nd	16:26
John	7th	16:45
Sam	10th	16:52
Bryce	12th	17:00
Top 5 Average		*16:38*

It was another solid team performance, and we matched our team average time from the previous week, even though we were running on a warm Friday afternoon. John, Sam and Bryce each ran well. Carlos and Jacob were both farther back than I would have expected. Carlos was especially disappointed since it was his birthday, and he was more motivated for this race than anyone else on the team. He may have even been too motivated. Kids with

able to match his personal best time of 15:50, which was only good enough for 23rd place in this stacked field of the state's best runners. From the top to the bottom of our lineup, our times were good, but our places were way too high.

Travis	23rd	15:50
Curtis	44th	16:10
Sam	65th	16:22
Bryce	90th	16:35
John	111th	16:49
Top 5 Average		*16:21*

In spite of the good times, our boys looked worried about where we'd finished in the team standings when I gathered them together after the race. They all realized that there were way too many bodies in front of us for the news about the team score to be very good. The results of a large cross country meet can be hard to figure, and official results often take what seems like an eternity to get posted.

One of my most notable memories of such a wait was at the 2000 State Meet in Titusville. Our Jesuit squad was ranked a distant 3rd entering the 2-A championship. Citrus High School was highly favored. There was a hard right turn about 80 meters from the finish line of that race, and I remember thinking we had no chance to win after 18 runners (including three from top-ranked Citrus) made that turn before our number one. Then something incredible started to happen. All year long, the gap between our number one and five runners was usually about 40 seconds, which is a pretty close spread. On this day, as soon as the first blue uniform made the turn, a pack of four more Jesuit harriers appeared almost right behind him.

All five of our scorers finished within six seconds of each other. To this day, I've never seen or heard of a team finishing with a tighter pack at a championship meet. As happy as we all were about the historic team finish, common sense told us that our tight pack was too far back to win the meet. I got so excited when our pack crossed the line that I forgot to pay attention to where Citrus's number four and five runners finished. I just assumed they had beaten us, but maybe our finish was good enough for second. I gathered the boys together, congratulated them on their valiant effort, and sent them on a cool down jog.

As I chatted with other 2-A coaches, no one seemed to know any more than I did about the team results. One coach told me that the fourth Citrus runner finished "in the 30s," and someone else said their fifth man was "much farther back." Each of our boys was given a place card when he finished, and our five places added up to 118 points. Historically, that team score is too high to win a state championship.

To make it more complex, the place on the cards that the runners get is not exactly the amount of points added to the team score. Some runners qualify for the State Meet as individuals, and their places are not counted in the team scoring. So just because another coach has five cards with a higher total, does not mean that you will beat that team when the non-scoring runners are removed.

After about an hour, runners and coaches gathered in the junior college gymnasium for the awards ceremony. After the excruciating wait, they finally began to announce the top ten 2-A teams, from tenth to first. When they got to fourth place, the announcer said, "With 120 points, Citrus High School." We were shocked. Citrus was the dominant 2-A team all year long. They were such a sure thing to win that their runners showed up to the starting line with their hair dyed in multi-colors as if their celebration had already begun.

"In third place . . . with 119 points . . . Bishop Moore."

With that announcement, there were two possible teams left, both named Jesuit. The Belen Jesuit crowd and the Tampa Jesuit crowd both waited nervously to hear the name of the runner-up. Neither side was anxious to hear their name just yet.

"Your 2000 2-A runner up . . . with 111 points . . . JESUIT!" The excitement in the announcer's voice was met with near-dead silence.

"Which Jesuit?" We all wondered anxiously.

"Sorry . . . That's 'Belen Jesuit' in second place," the announcer finally clarified. Loud, joyous cheers erupted from the fans in blue as the team in yellow came forward to accept the runner-up trophy.

After we exited the gymnasium, Linda was waiting with a cooler filled with several bottles of chilled, sparkling apple cider and some plastic champagne glasses. The boys took turns showering each other with the adolescent champagne, and then we all raised our glasses in a toast to the champions.

When the team results were finally posted at this year's 2011 Pre-State Meet, there was no such drama or joy. On the other hand, the team results were better than we had feared. We were 5th, just like we were in our first meet of the season. In fact, the same four teams that beat us at the Déjà Vu Meet beat us again (déjà vu?). Belen Jesuit was even more dominant than they were in September. This time, however, we cut the gap between us and the top two 4-A teams in half. Instead of being 17 and 29 seconds behind their team averages, we were 12 and 13 seconds back. Again, I was desperately hoping that we had already caught them, but getting halfway there on a day when I did not think we had run our best was encouraging.

If there has been a theme to our racing results this season, I guess you can say it's "meeting our expectations, but coming up short of our hopes." Our hard work was paying off, but would it be enough? We realized once again that realizing our dream was going to take more work than ever before. Our boys were up for the challenge. The best thing about this year's team is their willingness to continually increase their effort. That's exactly what we did in our next track workout the following Tuesday afternoon.

This time we didn't arrive at the track until 6 p.m. so we could have the track all to ourselves. The football team was exiting the field as we arrived, and I turned on the stadium lights, which gave us all the feeling that something special was about to happen. After a vigorous warm-up, the boys lined up at the top of the backstretch to begin the first of four 1,500-meter repeats. The last time we did 1,500-meter repeats at Al Lopez Park we did six, but we started out slowly and built up the speed with each one. This time we started super-fast to continue our efforts to prepare for a fast start at the State Meet.

Travis did the first one in 4:30 while Curtis was seven seconds back and the rest of the top seven were another eight seconds behind Curtis. The boys did a 500-meter jog and went right into the next repeat. On the second and third repeats, everybody was 15 seconds slower than the first with the same 500-meter jog recovery. On the final one, the boys were challenged to finish with their fastest 1500-meter repeat of the night. Six of our top seven were able to hit each repeat just as instructed. I was surprised there weren't more "casualties" during this workout. I was once again impressed by the high level of fitness in this group.

The Friday after that evening's track workout we had no school so I wanted to do something special with our varsity runners. We met at 7 a.m. at Plant, and I loaded the top 10 boys in a van to travel to Clermont, which is about 75 minutes east of Tampa. The city of Clermont is home to the U.S. National Training Center, and it also boasts the longest, steepest hills in Florida. We were introduced to Clermont by the Chamberlain team, who uses it as their summer camp site. We joined them for a two-day training retreat last January. The National Training Center features world class athletic facilities, and it attracts some of the nation's best athletes for testing, training and rehab from injuries.

Before we ever went to Clermont, we had heard of a 10-mile clay road loop that U.S. Olympian Ryan Hall had used for his training prior to the 2008 Games in Beijing. The clay loop starts on Five Mile Road, just off of Highway 27 in the heart of central Florida. The entire loop is on a wide red-clay road and surrounded by mostly undeveloped landscape that undulates in a way that is very uncharacteristic for Florida. The first five miles are mostly long, steady inclines on a single-lane road with only a few curves and virtually no traffic. At the five-mile mark the road ends (hence, the name) and runners turn right onto Schofield Road.

The next four miles feature dramatic changes in elevation and panoramic views. At one of the highest points on mile seven, runners can look down the long, steep hill and see one of Clermont's numerous beautiful lakes. The final mile is virtually flat, but still very difficult because it features loose sand that can suck the last bit of life from dying legs.

On this trip to Clermont, we were greeted by cool weather and clear skies. I put the boys into two groups and told them to start off easy and then start a series of 15-minute "pick-ups," followed by 10 minutes of recovery running. After they started, I drove the van in the opposite direction on the loose dirt of the final mile and parked somewhere near the nine-mile mark before I started my own run going in a counterclockwise direction opposite of the boys.

I was thoroughly enjoying the cool, clear air and the beautiful scenery as I ran as easily as I could up the steep trail. I ran for about 30 minutes and then turned around in the hopes of beating the boys to the nine-mile mark where the van was parked. I picked up my pace a bit on the way back, but when I got to the top of the hill at the seven-mile mark with the beautiful lake view, I had to slow to a walk to take it all in. I took time to appreciate the beautiful scenery and the incredible group of young men who could very easily be 60 miles away from here asleep in their warm, cozy beds. This kind of moment is what might just keep me in coaching a while longer.

Once I got to the lake at the bottom of that long hill, I turned and looked back up the hill from which I had just descended to see if I could spot the lead group of the top seven runners. Sure enough, there they were starting their descent. It dawned on me that they probably have no idea how wonderfully amazing and special it is to be able to do what they were doing. I know from experience that most of them won't realize this until later in their lives. Many of them will never be able to use their bodies this effortlessly ever again. Even the ones that go on to run in college will eventually realize the special nature of being on a high school team like ours. Some will try to re-live the experience in various ways by joining running clubs or other athletic groups as adults, but nothing can replace the experience of being part of a team on a valiant quest for a magical State Championship.

When the lead group came running by me, they offered me encouragement. "Good job, Coach," they hollered out to me as they passed. They were all smiling and running smoothly as they passed me—all but one. I only counted six bodies as they went by. I looked back, and I could see Sam well behind his teammates. The boys flew by so fast that I could not ask them if Sam was alright. I started to worry that this beautiful day was going to be spoiled by an injury to one of our top runners. Sam's knee had bothered him earlier in the season, but after a couple of weeks of limiting the mileage and intensity of his workouts, it cleared up. As he got closer I started to realize that he was moving at a pretty good pace. I figured that was a good sign.

"Bryce kicked off my shoe," he said to me with a smile as he flew by me on his way to the group ahead. To say I breathed a sigh of relief is an understatement.

The second group caught me just before I got to the van. They also looked smooth and comfortable though they were farther behind the lead group than I would have expected. When I drove the van back to the point where the boys had started their run, I figured out why there was such a huge gap between the two groups. Travis approached me and showed me his watch, which read 1 hour and 34 minutes. The boys had averaged under 6:30 per mile for their ten mile run.

"We were flying," they proudly reported to me. We hopped back into the van and headed to the nearby Cracker Barrel restaurant for a well-deserved feast of down-home country cooking.

The final regular-season meet of the year for us was the Hillsborough County Championships on the Tuesday following our evening track workout. The main competition for us this year looked to be the Steinbrenner Warriors. This school, named after the famed owner of the New York Yankees, the late George Steinbrenner, is only in its third year of existence and already emerging as a force to be reckoned with in cross country. Last year they took runner-up at the 2-A State Meet, and this year, even with the loss of a couple of key scorers, they seem to be even better.

The key to Steinbrenner's meteoric rise in the cross country ranks is coaching. The head coach, Bobby McConnell, was a standout runner at Leto during the glory days when they were Hillsborough County's dominant program, earning seven state championships in the 1980s and 90s. The coach of that legendary program, known as the Long Red Row, was my friend Bobby Ennis, who also happens to be teaching physical education at Steinbrenner. Though he threatens to quit if he gets referred to publically as the coach, everyone who follows our sport closely knows that he is busy working the same magic he did two decades ago.

To give even more credibility to the Warrior coaching staff, the only other coach in Florida with more state titles in boys cross country than Bobby Ennis, the legendary Brent Haley who came to help Travis beat the "Bear," has also been working with the team. Bobby and Brent became best friends after spending over a decade as arch rivals. To have both of them on the same staff is an incredible advantage. It still comes down to teenage boys doing the work, and the Steinbrenner boys have done their work.

Drama started early at the County Championship when we all realized that it was 30 minutes past the time that I had asked the boys to show up, and Curtis, our number-two runner, was still not there. I called him just before the JV race was about to start, and he said he was lost. When I asked him what road he was on, he said he was on I-275. That was very bad news. We were already missing Jacob, a usual top-5 runner for us, who was suffering from the flu.

If Curtis was on I-275, that meant he probably got directions for Lettuce Lake Park instead of Lake Park. It wouldn't have been the first time that mistake has happened. I had warned the boys several times to make sure they went to "Lake Park" which is on the far west of town and not "Lettuce Lake Park" which is on the far east of Tampa. I even explained to them that the race course was on the same road as our school, Dale Mabry Highway, just about 15 miles north of us. He eventually arrived just as the others were starting the warm-up.

Travis was ranked third among the runners in the varsity race. The heavy favorite to win the individual title was Max del Monte of Chamberlain, who was highly recruited by several top schools before accepting a scholarship to run at FSU. Max and Travis have become friends over the past year, and they did several training runs together over the summer. They talked about their race strategy the day before the meet, and they decided to work together in the first half of the race and run an even pace early on. The plan was for them to go through the mile mark at about 5:05 and then make a surge going into the second mile.

When I first saw them after the start, it was right after the mile mark, and they were starting their surge. To me, it looked like Travis was running as fast as he could to stay with Max, and I started to worry that the big move might take too much out of him. The pair started to pull away from the third place runner, Michael Babinec, from Riverview High School. Babinec was someone that Travis had previously been unable to beat. When I saw them again

109

about a half-mile later, Travis was still in contact with Max, but the Riverview runner had matched their surge and caught back up to them. The three were now well ahead of the rest of the field.

The remainder of the Plant runners all seemed a bit farther back than I expected by that point. Steinbrenner had three runners in front of our second runner and their four and five runners were keeping pace with the heart of our pack. It was an aggressive strategy by the Steinbrenner runners. Though it was still early in the race, I was getting plenty nervous.

The next time I saw the boys was at about the two-and-a half-mile mark. The front pack of three runners was still well in front, and Max and Travis had a small gap of two or three meters over Babinec. Steinbrenner still had three runners in front of our number two runner, but Curtis had closed the gap on their number three, who had fallen a bit behind his top two teammates. John and Sam were just behind Curtis, and Bryce was a few seconds back, right in front of Steinbrenner's four and five runners. My head was spinning too fast to try to do the math, but at this point, it seemed like a virtual tie.

I had told our boys that if we put all five scorers in the top 20 we would win the meet. Bryce was right at the 20th position, but the outcome seemed anything but certain. Max and Travis pulled away from Babinec in the final 400 meters as I was sprinting toward a spot where I could get a view of the finish. Max won the race in 15:13, but Travis stayed close, finishing in second place just three seconds back in 15:16. Curtis did not achieve his goal of finishing in the top ten, but he did eventually pass the number three Steinbrenner runner to finish in 13th place. John and Sam were right behind Steinbrenner's number three in 15th and 16th place. Although Bryce held on to 20th place, he got outkicked at the finish line by Steinbrenner's number four man.

The times were super-fast because the actual distance was closer to three miles than 5K due to flooding issues on the course.

Travis	2nd	15:16
Curtis	13th	16:05
John	15th	16:15
Sam	16th	16:17
Bryce	20th	16:25
Top 5 Average		*16:03*

It was too close to call. We would have to wait for the official results to be sure, but I was starting to prepare myself to be the victim of a major upset. "I think they got us," I said when I saw Jordan, one of my assistant coaches.

"I think they did too," he said with a shocked look on his face.

This was not what I was hoping to hear. I sent the boys on a cool down run and I went to the scorer's table to await the results. Even with the chip timing we use now, it still seems to take forever to get final results. I was watching the scorer's computer screen when he clicked the final button to make the results appear.

"Shit!" It was out of my mouth before I had time to consider my surroundings.

We were third. Third!? Steinbrenner was first, Berkeley Prep was second, and we were third. I was in disbelief. Within a couple of seconds, however, there was a glimmer of hope. "Did you only run six runners tonight?" the scorer asked me.

"No. We had a full team of seven," I replied with hopeful anticipation.

Then Jordan spoke up. "I bet it was John. His chip came off during the race, but he was afraid to tell you."

The funny thing is, before almost every race I say the same stupid rhyme—"Remember fellas, loose laces lose races." It's usually more for their pre-race amusement than anything else. After all these years, it finally proved to be true . . . at least for short while.

We had to do some investigative work to establish his time and place before he could be manually entered into the results. When all of that was finally done, the button was pushed once more, and this time we were the county champions.

As we walked back to our team area from the scorer's table, Bryan, my other young assistant said, "I've never won a county championship before, but somehow I thought it would be more fun." Those words are still resonating with me. The whole afternoon had felt more frustrating than fun. Why are we working so hard if it's not going to be fun even when we win in the end?

The lesson from this meet was not to underestimate a worthy opponent. When I met with the boys the next day to sum up the meet, I simply told them the truth. "Plant showed up in khaki pants and button-down shirts for a race while Steinbrenner arrived with their shirts off ready for a fight," I said. In the end, our boys did rise to meet the challenge, and they did find a way to win. The bad news is that Steinbrenner returns virtually their entire varsity next year, while we will lose five of our top seven. The County Championship is going to be one tough title to defend. For now though, it's ours—and our boys earned every bit of it.

The Plant Panther Boys celebrate their
2011 County Championship
Left to right: Carlos, Joe, Anatoly, Curtis, Bryce, Travis, John, Sam
and Jacob
(Photo courtesy of Natalie Cheeseman)

Chapter Eleven

CHAMPIONSHIP MONTH

November 2011

November is championship month for high school cross country teams in Florida. This is the time of year that we have been dreaming about and planning for since last May. Near the end of any race, onlookers can see that some runners time their kick just right, accelerating past other runners all the way through the finish line. Other runners seem to be holding on for dear life as the finish line nears. Their bodies start to tie up, their pace slows and they helplessly watch opponents fly on by. It's all about pace and timing. So it is with the season. Some teams are just starting to peak, and they will go flying through November, beating teams that peaked too soon.

As for my own running, I don't think there's much danger of me peaking too early. The climax of the cross country season has forced me to put my own running in the back seat while I focused on preparing my team for their final surge. My mileage total for the month of November slipped to 125 miles. Still, my weekend long runs continued to progress well. Two weeks after our 20-mile October finale that included the magical dolphin encounter, Greg and I set out for an 18-mile run on virtually the same course minus a two-mile out-and-back at the tip of Davis Island.

About 300 meters from the end of the Bayshore I began thinking about meeting "Flipper" two weeks earlier, and I started to ponder whether it was even remotely possible to see our young dolphin again. Even as I was trying to push that ridiculous thought out of my head, a small fin appeared within 30 meters of the Bayshore seawall. Could it possibly be "our" dolphin? Again, Greg missed the first appearance.

"He's back to run with us," I said to Greg excitedly.

Both of us started calling out to "Flipper" and we slapped our hands on the top of the seawall as we ran slowly with our eyes fixed down into the bay. Greg even started making dolphin noises, which actually sounded more like prolonged kisses. Within seconds our dolphin was right there swimming along the seawall and keeping pace with us once again.

As if it weren't enough that this improbable scene was repeating itself, it quickly got even better. The first time we met this dolphin, the water was clear enough to see his whole body, but only his fin broke the surface. This time, he lifted his head above the surface of the water as if to get a better look at us.

"Holy shit," I said to Greg. "He's looking right at us."

The second encounter lasted twice as long as the first, and any doubt I had about the mutual nature of the relationship was gone. The only question left in my mind was whether he remembered us from the previous encounter. I'm not much of an animal person, and I have often accused pet lovers of projecting their own thoughts and emotions onto their beloved animals. So many dog and cat owners come to believe that their pets are different from all other animals and that their relationship is really more than just a series of conditioned responses. No doubt that's exactly what I am doing with Flipper. But still, maybe MY pet really IS special . . .

The Sunday before our second Flipper encounter, Greg and I traveled to Clermont to run the 10-mile clay loop where I took my team in October. Greg had never run this loop. When I first mentioned it to him, he wasn't convinced that 10 miles would be enough mileage. Once we started climbing the long, steep hills and the soft clay began sucking the life out of our legs, he was more than satisfied with a 10-mile Sunday run. Two weeks later we ran 12 miles on the far less hilly roads of Temple Terrace. What made that run especially difficult was that it was the day after the State Championship meet and both of us were physically, mentally and emotionally spent.

The Florida Cross Country Championship Series consists of three stages. Schools are divided into four classifications based on school population (1-A through 4-A). Each of those classes is divided into 16 districts. District championship meets are held during the first week of November. The top three or four teams (depending on the size of the district) qualify for the region meet held the next week while the season ends for teams who do not qualify. Each class then holds four region meets for the 12 to 16 qualifying teams. The top six teams from each of those region meets qualify for the State Championship Meet held on the third Saturday in November.

This year our team was part of a seven-team district that featured no state-ranked teams other than ours. In fact, our second-best seven runners who won the Brandon meet in October would have been the odds-on favorite to win the team title in this district. Given the relative lack of competition at our district meet, I decided to use this race as an opportunity to practice an aggressive strategy that we might want to use at the State Meet to match up with the hard-charging Columbus boys, who like to get out very quickly at big meets.

In our previous two meetings against Columbus this season, their boys were able to quickly put a large gap between their pack and ours. The Columbus boys would eventually slow their pace some, but the number of runners between their pack and ours was so large that we were unable to pass enough bodies to catch back up to them. This aggressive kind of racing is not supposed to work in cross country races, but they've used it successfully to win three straight titles.

Evenly paced racing, or something close to it, is supposed to be the optimal way to race. But since this is what we were up against, I decided we would use this district meet to find out if we could successfully employ a more aggressive strategy that would give us a chance to match up with the Columbus boys from the beginning, and then stick with them. It's hard to beat them if you can never see them.

Plant was the host school for the district meet, and once again, I was in charge of putting on the meet at the Ed Radice Soccer Complex, where we ran the season-opening Déjà Vu meet. When I announced my plan for hosting this meet, several coaches were less than happy with my choice of site. Some coaches only know this course as the site of the season-opening mud-fest with slow times and lost shoes. These coaches don't remember that this course was once the site of the State Meet, and it became synonymous with blazing fast times on a super-fast, super-flat course. By November, the soft, wet soccer fields become hard and dry, and the cool evening temperatures are just right for running fast.

It was on one of these electric nights in 2003 that I witnessed the best display of evenly paced racing I've ever seen. At the Pre-State Meet earlier that season, Andy Biladeau, our top Jesuit runner at the time, had his worst race of the season on that same Ed Radice course. We concluded that he had been too aggressive. A couple of weeks prior to the 2003 State Meet, we went to Ed Radice for practice, and I painted marks on the course at each kilometer. We estimated that he would need to run about 15:20 to win the championship race, so we practiced running one-kilometer repeats at 3:04. On race night, when the leaders hit the mile mark, Andy was well back in the pack, and many assumed he was having another off night. Instead, his steady pacing took him to the front of the pack shortly after the two mile, and he cruised to a stunning victory in 15:21, splitting each kilometer in almost exactly 3:04.

Nobody ran anywhere near that fast at our 2011 District Meet. We ran the District Meet without Bryce in the lineup. He began complaining about pain in his shins a few days before the meet. We gave him a couple of days off from running and decided to let him run in the open race prior to the varsity race so that he could feel free to drop out if it got too painful. This gave Joe a chance to break into the top seven. He had a breakthrough race in the junior varsity division at County Meet (with another one of his patented "Crazy Joe" screaming finishes) and earned a chance to run head-to-head for a place in our lineup.

The plan called for our entire top seven to get out super-quick and stick with Travis for the first half-mile. From that point, Travis was supposed to stick with Curtis and help him break the 16-minute barrier. The rest of the guys were supposed to stay packed up as long as possible and keep the gap between themselves and Curtis as small as possible. What I didn't expect was for Travis to go out even quicker than usual for the first half-mile. This meant that the pace went from "aggressive" to "insane" for the rest of the boys.

The week prior to our District Meet we went out to the Ed Radice course for practice, and we rehearsed the first kilometer of the race by doing five one-kilometer repeats from the start line of the race. During each repeat, the boys hit the half-mile mark between 2:26 to 2:28, just under a five-minute mile pace. After the gun went off to start the District Meet, the boys hit that same half-mile mark between 2:20 to 2:22, much faster than they did in practice. Our top seven were already several meters in front of the entire field. Unfortunately, some of them already looked like they were hanging on for dear life.

Travis and Curtis came through the mile in 4:54. For some reason, Travis put in a surge just past the mile mark and put a gap between himself and Curtis. I was confused and frustrated by Travis's move. Apparently, Travis had told Curtis that he would be making a move at the mile mark to avoid slowing down during the second mile. It was a logical thought, but it didn't take into account that Curtis would need to slow down a bit to recover from the first mile. By the time Travis got to the second mile, Curtis was hopelessly off the pace and barely hanging on.

The rest of the team slowly and steadily got separated from each other. The race devolved into the kind of "every man for himself" effort that was the last thing I wanted to see happen. Luckily, our boys were strong enough to hang on to the top five places, giving us a dominating victory with a perfect team score of 15. Our top five included:

Travis	1st	16:03
John	2nd	16:45
Curtis	3rd	16:52
Sam	4th	17:17
Jacob	5th	17:22
Top 5 Average		*16:52*

To the untrained eye, our team ran a great race. Scoring fifteen points in a cross country meet is like rolling a perfect score of 300 in bowling. To a veteran observer, however, the Panthers looked vulnerable. This is why my good friend, the legendary Brent Haley, phoned me the next day with some friendly advice.

"I know you think you gotta get out really quick to beat Columbus, but I gotta tell you, Mike, I believe that'd be a big mistake." Coach Haley apologized profusely for second-guessing our race strategy. I assured him that, not only did I appreciate his opinion, but I had already come to the same conclusion. If our district race would have included more competitive teams, they could have easily taken advantage of the way our team was spread out and our boys were slowing down in the final stretch. Going out hard was worth a try, but it was too late to start trying something so far out of our comfort zone. Our best chance to pull off an upset would be to run our own race strategy to the best of our ability. After the District Meet, however, our upset chances seemed to be dimming.

The Region Meet was scheduled to be run in Sarasota, eight days after the district race. Once again we would be the favored team, but this time there would be a handful of other state-ranked teams who would be aiming to take us down. The team with the best shot to beat our boys was Seminole. This is the team that narrowly beat us in the camp race in July. Their team is dominated by a talented and veteran group of seniors who were very motivated to send off their beloved, long-time coach, Bruce Calhoun, into retirement with a championship.

The only time we ran head-to-head with Seminole during the season was at the Pre-State Meet where they finished with a team average that was 13 seconds slower than ours. On one hand, that seemed like a pretty safe margin between our two teams. But after the scare we got from Steinbrenner at the County Meet, we knew better than to take Seminole lightly, especially considering the Seminole boys beat Steinbrenner at Pre-State.

There was another team with ample talent and motivation to win the Region Meet. Vero Beach won their district with blazing fast times that made them appear to be contenders for the region championship and perhaps even an upset at the State Meet. Like our county meet, these extraordinarily fast times raised several eyebrows, and eventually the results were entered in the flrunners. com database as three-mile times rather than 5K. This prompted the usual protests and arguments on the Internet running forum among coaches, runners and parents.

"Wait until you see what we do in Sarasota," one Vero Beach supporter posted on the running forum in response to those who doubted the legitimacy of their district times.

There is always some question in my mind as to how important it really is to win the Region Meet. If we were to focus solely on having the best chance to win the State Meet, it might be best to run a more controlled race at the Region Meet in order to leave more in the tank for the State Meet. But then there's the psychological factor. How do you ask kids to run less than their best when their competitors are giving everything they've got to beat them?

As much as I've thought about this strategy over the years, I can't remember a time that our team could have won the Region Meet but didn't because we were saving up for state. There were a few years when our team was so dominant that we won the region without an all-out effort, but that's very different from conceding a victory.

One thing was certain, our race strategy would be very different than it was at the District Meet. We studied the region field carefully, paying particular attention to the Seminole boys to determine what it was going to take to get the victory. Like the County Meet, we were dealing with a highly motivated competitor, and that can make a huge difference. We learned our lesson from our cliff-hanger experience against Steinbrenner. This time we talked about the fact that the second half of the race was going to be a "fight." Each of our boys went into the race ready to run a conservative first mile, use the second mile to locate and match up with specific competitors, and then do everything they could to battle their way in front of the Seminole boys.

The conservative first mile part of the strategy turned out to be harder for the back end of our pack than we expected. The Region Meet course gets very narrow very quickly, and our five through seven runners found themselves farther back than we wanted them to be after the start. Once the course entered the long, narrow trails, they were struggling to get past slower runners who were blocking the path as our main competitors opened a wide lead. Eventually, all of our boys found their way to the right place in the pack, but not without expending significant energy trying to get there.

At the halfway point, Travis was in third place and sitting right on Seminole's number one runner, Jacob Hudak. This was right where we agreed he should be until the final mile. Curtis, John and Sam were positioned right between Seminole's two and three runners, which is what we planned. What I did not expect was that Seminole's number four was also right behind that group and well in front of the rest of our boys. Jacob, Carlos and Bryce were back a few places battling with Seminole's five and six runners.

"Yikes!" I said to myself as I sprinted toward the two mile mark. "This is gonna be really close."

When Travis reached the two-mile mark he made the surge that we had planned, passed Hudak and started to close on the leader, Michael Babinec, the runner Travis finally beat at the County Meet. Curtis and John were both in the top 10 and still battling with Seminole's two and three runners. Sam had fallen a few meters back and was locked in a battle with Seminole's number four. Seminole's five and six runners were sitting on Carlos, who was now our fifth man. Bryce was chasing Seminole's five and six. Though Bryce was well enough to be back in the lineup for this meet, he was clearly not back to top form yet. Jacob was struggling mightily, and it appeared he would not be able to figure in the scoring.

I sprinted back to a spot that was about 500 meters from the finish and waited for the boys to emerge from the wooded trails and enter the final stretch. The first uniform I saw was orange—Seminole's color. It was Hudak, and he was all alone. Clearly he had come back with a surge of his own. A few seconds passed before I saw the second uniform emerge—blue. It was Babinec. Eventually, a black and gold uniform appeared, and Travis emerged in third place. He didn't look sharp.

The Seminole and Plant packs soon emerged, and the boys were in exactly the kind of dogfight we anticipated. Curtis was shoulder to shoulder with Seminole's number two, and John was not far behind. Seminole's number three was chasing after John, while Sam was still locked in a tight battle with Seminole's fourth. Seminole's five and six were now in front of Carlos.

"They've got us," I thought to myself.

The runners entered onto a track for 150 meters before briefly disappearing into wooded trails at the far end and then re-appearing before making pair of sharp turns and starting the final 80-meter sprint. Travis made it home safely in third. Curtis accelerated past Seminole's number two and finished in sixth place. John finished right behind Seminole's number two in eighth place. Somehow, Sam, who looked like he was spent with 500 meters to go, not only won the battle with Seminole's number four, but he then sprinted past Seminole's number three just before crossing the finish line.

Each team now had four runners across the line, and there was a significant gap between both team's four and five runners. Luckily, Carlos not only stayed with Seminole's five and six, he also put in a furious sprint to catch and then pass them both just before the finish line. Carlos's kick saved the day. The Panther boys won by a mere three points. The final score was Plant 48, Seminole 51. It was a hard-fought, narrow victory over a talented and motivated team.

The host of the meet recognized Coach Calhoun during the awards ceremony and gave him a gift to honor his many years of dedicated service to his sport and his runners. My heart went out to him, but I know he had to be proud of the way his boys gave everything they had to beat us. The Vero Beach boys finished a distant third with 95 points. All of the times were slow on the narrow, winding course.

Travis	3rd	16:31
Curtis	6th	16:57
John	8th	16:58
Sam	11th	17:07
Carlos	24th	17:45
Top 5 Average		*17:04*

On the positive side, the heart of our lineup (Curtis, John and Sam) ran great. Travis was not at his best, however, and the gap between four and five made us very vulnerable. A gap like that at the State Meet would take us out of the top five for sure.

We had done our final hard track workout of the season on the Tuesday before the Region Meet. It consisted of a fast 1K, followed by a 3K at tempo pace, a 2K at race pace, and then a final fast 1K. It was the first time all year that Travis didn't hit every split the way I instructed. It was a hard workout, which is what I wanted nearly two weeks from the State Meet, but probably the reason that he was not at his best at the Region Meet. I was confident Travis would bounce back. I was also confident that the heart of our lineup was peaking at just the right time. I was nervous that, without a fifth runner much closer to the middle of our pack, the State Meet could end in bitter disappointment.

In the final two weeks of the season we cut back our total mileage by about 30 percent, but the percentage of the miles run at a "quality" pace actually increased. After the final big track workout on the Tuesday before the Region Meet, we didn't do anything that pushed the runners' limits. We did try to do enough faster running to maintain the boys' sense of fitness while maintaining fresh legs. "Fit, fresh and fast," was our mantra for the final week of training before the state meet.

Something else that seemed to develop in the final two weeks was a realistic sense of acceptance of the fact that our fate was not completely in our own hands. We could not control how other runners performed. We agreed to focus on giving our best possible performance. I had worked these boys harder than any of my previous teams, and they rose to every challenge. No one said it explicitly, but we all knew that if either Colonial or Columbus ran to their potential, it would be nearly impossible to beat either of them.

"The biggest tragedy," I told our boys, "would be if either of those teams has an off day, and we don't run well enough to take advantage of it." Also implied in that tragic scenario would be the disappointment of getting beat by any of the teams ranked behind us.

I used Travis as an example. With all of the top ten boys gathered around me after an easy Bayshore run a couple of days before the state meet, I bluntly asked the boys, "Do you expect Travis to win the meet?" There was a pause. Everybody was afraid to speak the obvious truth. As I would have expected, Carlos was the first to speak up.

"No. Not really," he said to me with confidence in front of his older teammates.

"Why not? Don't you think he's going to give everything he can to win the race?" I baited him.

"Because I don't think he can beat Arroyo." Carlos answered as he smiled sheepishly in Travis's direction.

Andres Arroyo was the odds-on favorite to win the individual 4-A state championship. He was arguably the best runner in any classification, and no one in our class had even given him a close race all year. Most onlookers who offered predictions about our race ranked Travis anywhere from sixth to eleventh, depending on what method they were using to rank the runners. Even if Arroyo got sick during the race, Travis would have to beat at least half-a-dozen runners whom he had previously never beaten to claim the title.

"Are any of you gonna be disappointed in Travis if he doesn't win?" I asked with a wry smile.

This time the answer was swift and unanimous as the group responded with a strong, choral "NO!"

I wanted to make sure my point was very clear, so I persisted. "Why won't you be disappointed? He's going out there to win, and if he doesn't win, he's failed. So why won't you be disappointed in him?"

Another pause—I suspected that each boy had some intuitive sense of the answer, but once again the boys left it up to the youngest member of the top seven to put it into words.

"Because he can only do the best he can do. He can't control what the other runners do. If he hasn't beaten another kid all year, we can't get mad at him if he doesn't beat him on Saturday."

I explained to the boys that, as much as I would cherish another state championship, I could only expect them to do the best that they could do. I think they understood, but of course I was talking as much (or more?) to myself as I was to them. It had been a long six months and a whole lot of dreaming, planning and work was spent to achieve a single goal. Now, barring some miracle, it seemed that the ultimate goal might just elude us. It was time to start putting it all into a healthy perspective.

Nobody on the Internet message boards was giving us a chance. Predictions on the 4-A team competition were evenly split between Columbus and Colonial. From a psychological standpoint, most athletes would rather be in the role of David than Goliath. Everyone expects Goliath to win. When he does win, that's not even news. No one expects David to win. If he fights valiantly and loses, there is no shame. If, by some miracle, he should win, it's an epic tale.

Our problem was that there were two Goliaths. Our only hope was that they would each beat each other up to the point where we could seize the opportunity to defeat even one of them. Or, maybe, they would each be so focused on the other that we could sneak by both of them.

A welcome sense of peace came over me in the final days leading up to the State Meet. So many things this season went much better than they had gone in recent years. Two years ago I was seriously questioning myself as a coach when injuries mounted up, and I started to wonder if pursuing state championships was really worth the effort and risks involved. I vowed to work these boys harder than any previous team of mine, and I did. This year's team has given me new hope and a renewed sense of the value of what we get for our sacrifices—win or lose.

Our boys showed up at the State Meet healthy and ready. Even Bryce seemed back up to speed. He was able to put in a full week of practice without pain. John asked for a few minutes to address the guys before the race, so we agreed he would do that about 20 minutes before the start. I sent the boys on a 15-minute run about an hour before the race to get them loosened up a bit. The boys threw in a one-minute surge near the end of that warm-up run to get their hearts and lungs ready for the shock that was coming soon.

The girls' race started 40 minutes before our race, so they had just finished when I gathered the boys up for John to address the team. Two Plant girls were in the top six, which was better than expected. Our fourth and fifth girls, however, were a bit farther back than expected. Although it was too close to call, it seemed that our girls ran well, and maybe well enough to repeat as state champions. There was no time to worry about that now, though, as the event we had been anticipating for months was only minutes away.

"I just want to say that I'm really glad I gave up football to join this team," John started. "I'm really proud to be a part of this team, and you can count on me to set a good pace for our pack that will put us all in the position we need to be in. At the halfway point, Curtis is going to make his move, and we all need to stay as close as possible to each other to have a chance to win."

We were really lucky that John left football to join our team. Though we had a good group of seniors, none of the others had his outgoing, extraverted, can-do type of personality.

Travis spoke next. "I came here to win today—not to get second or third," he began. "Don't give in when it starts to get hard. Just remember your teammates and know that, if we all give everything we've got, we can win this." So much for our talk on the

Bayshore a few days earlier, I thought to myself. Just when I thought we were all on board with the idea that giving our best was good enough, my team captain decides only winning is good enough. I was very proud of him. I had done my job, now he was doing his.

I sent the boys down to the starting line to begin their pre-race warm-up drills. I met them there about 10 minutes later, and we went over the race plan one last time. Travis needed to get out quickly and settle in behind the lead pack. John was going to lead the rest of the team up the first hill quickly but without sprinting out too hard. By the half-mile mark, John was to take an outside position and slowly start moving our pack into a competitive position. We needed to be far enough up so that Curtis would have a chance to make it into the top 20 by the end of the race. We hoped to get John and Sam into the top 30, and we needed our fifth runner to maintain the closest possible contact.

At the midway point of the race, things looked good for our boys. Travis was in sixth place, and only the top two runners had any sizable gap on him. He was part of a chase-pack of six runners and looked fairly comfortable. John and Curtis were in good position. Curtis started to make his surge forward just as we planned and was already in the top 30 with several runners in striking distance ahead of him. John looked strong and was holding a spot somewhere between 30th and 40th. Sam was struggling a little, but he also had a decent position at about the 50th spot.

The big question was our fifth man. If we left this gap open like we did at the Region Meet, we'd be doomed. Fortunately, it looked as if Bryce was ready to fill that gap. He was only about 10 places behind Sam and looking strong. Jacob was only 10 to 15 places behind Bryce. I stood near the exit which leads the runners back onto the track from which they would have one kilometer to go.

The first figure I saw flying down the hill toward me was Arroyo. No one was going to catch him today. The next uniform I saw belonged to a Buchholz runner who qualified as an individual. That was also to be expected. The real surprise came next as Travis came flying down the hill in third place, and he actually seemed to be gaining some ground on the second-place runner only 30 to 40 meters ahead. Holy Cow!

I loudly counted out places as the runners sped by. When I saw Curtis, I shouted out "YOU'RE 25! Five more places to go! GOOO! GET 'EM!"

John was about 10 to 15 places back, and Sam was somewhere between 50 to 60. Not too bad. The best news was that Bryce was closing on Sam and now only about five places behind him. Jacob was another 20 or so places back.

The announcer soon brought the crowd's attention to Arroyo and urged everyone to "bring him home under 15 minutes." When I looked at the clock and then back at Arroyo, I knew there was no way he was going to crack 15 minutes the way he did at the Pre-State Meet. It's not that he wasn't giving the same kind of effort, but the conditions were not quite as good as they were at Pre-State, and he had no one to push him like he did a month earlier when the top runners from the other three classifications were on his heels.

I could see that the Buchholz runner was still safely in second. He had re-opened his gap on Travis. In fact, by the time Travis passed me with about 80 meters left, he was in fifth place with a sixth runner in hot pursuit. Then came the greatest kick of Travis's career. He went into another gear to take fourth and eventually third place just before crossing the finish line in a personal and school record time of 15:42.

When I looked back down the "Green Monster," which is how this year's announcer was referring to the long uphill finish, I soon spotted Curtis. He had made it all the way up to 20th position by the time he reached me, and then he managed to outkick a couple more runners before crossing the line.

John was next. Though he did not get into the top 30, he was close. By this point the density of bodies crossing in front me was growing, and it became nearly impossible to maintain an accurate count, but it was not too long before Sam and then Bryce came by me. Both were looking good and still moving well, competing for every last spot. Jacob also looked strong as he started his sprint to the finish

Six good races. It was probably not enough to win on this day, but a huge accomplishment nonetheless. My experience in state meets has taught me that, though some kids will breakthrough with a well-timed season-best as Travis did, it's far more common for kids to stretch themselves a bit too far and pay the price with a sub-par performance. The results of this meet would later confirm my experience, as there were far more teams and individuals who fell short of expectations than those who exceeded them.

Even as I entered the area where the runners exit the course, I could overhear coaches and onlookers speculating about the team results. There seemed to be a growing consensus that Colonial had beaten Columbus. One of the first faces I saw as I entered the finish area was the young Colonial coach who was wearing a cautious, but unmistakable smile.

"You think you got it, Coach?" I asked as we shook hands.

"I really hope so," he replied. "These kids *really* deserve this."

He was right. As much as I wanted to see our boys as David in this struggle, it was really the Colonial boys who played that part all along. Columbus is the largest private school in the state, with numerous state titles in various sports. Colonial is just another big metro-area public school with no great sports tradition and no state titles in any sport—ever. Coach Placencia and his Colonial boys were devastated after losing to Columbus the previous year and, with all seven runners returning this season, had put everything they had into preventing Columbus from winning a fourth consecutive title.

Soon after shaking Coach Placencia's hand, I saw Coach Fleitas from Columbus. His face said it all before he did. "They got us this time," he said to me as we shook hands.

But, what about our Plant boys? I wondered to myself as I gathered our guys together. In all of my desperate attempts to count the places as the boys ran by me at the finish, I never really noticed where any other team was positioned other than ours. Clearly, most folks believed Colonial to have the lowest score, but I knew our score couldn't be too high. When I finally gathered all of our boys together, I was very quick to stress how proud and happy I was with the way our team ran. Though I could see how disappointed Carlos was, I knew even he could appreciate what a good day it had been for our team as a whole.

I told the boys that most people seemed to think that Colonial ran a great race and had the lowest score, but other than that we would have to wait for the official results. I congratulated them on a great team race, and I especially praised the way they were able to finish strong up the final hill to take some key positions in the final stretch.

"I don't know where we are going to finish in the team standings," I told them, "but Travis broke the school 5K record, and our point total has got to be the lowest since I have been at Plant."

We walked back to our team camp with our heads held high—all except Carlos. He stopped me before we reached the team camp, and he got emotional as he apologized for his disappointing performance.

"It wasn't your fault, Carlos." I assured him. "You gave everything you had. You are just a sophomore, yet I pushed you just as hard as all those older kids. You just peaked too early, that's all." I reminded him of how far he'd come since his freshman cross country season and how valuable he was to our team, not just as a runner, but as a leader. I reminded him of his best races in mid-season, and the way his great kick had clinched the Region Meet victory. Finally, I assured him that next year we would learn from this experience, and he would hit his peak in November the way his older teammates had done this season.

By the time we got to the team camp, Carlos was smiling. Soon, we all got news that made us smile even bigger. The Plant girls had won another state title. Coach Harrison's team earned him his tenth championship—tying him with Coach Haley for the most state titles of any single-gender coach. We quickly carted the cooler with the sparkling apple cider down to the girls' camp and proceeded to spray the screaming girls with sugary suds. On the way back to our own camp, we got more good news. When I finally saw Coach Harrison and congratulated him, he said, "Your guys got third."

I hurried up to see the official team results. Here are the top 4-A teams:

1st	Colonial	86 points	16:06 avg.
2nd	Columbus	103 points	16:19 avg.
3rd	HB Plant	146 points	16:27 avg.
4th	Seminole	163 points	16:30 avg.

I was very happy to see that the only team that even came close to taking the third spot away from us was Seminole. Those kids made yet another heroic attempt to send their beloved Coach Calhoun into retirement as a champion. I was genuinely happy for him and his team.

When I got back to the team camp I gathered all of the Plant runners, parents and supporters around to share the news. The first thing that popped into my mind as I summed up the day's events was how truly happy I was that so many of our JV runners showed up to be a part of this day. Going to Little Everglades Ranch to watch our State Meet is no simple task. It's far, it's expensive, and it's early. Having so many of our JV boys there gave me great hope for the future of our program and great confidence that the boys are really buying into the fact that there is great value in what we are doing.

I said to those who were gathered, "The first time we saw Columbus this year they beat us by nearly 20 seconds, the second time they got us by 13 seconds, and this time we were just 8 seconds away from defeating the three-time defending state champs for the runner-up spot." Then I reminded them that we were, in fact, champions. "In the past month we have won the County Championship, the District Championship and the Region Championship."

Then I turned my attention to Travis. For some reason, I started to get emotional as I tried to put his historic effort into perspective. "In all the many years that Plant High School has been around," I told them, "no one has ever run a faster 5K cross country race than Travis did today."

The boys all got some well-deserved applause from those gathered around us. We all hugged and posed for photos. I went over and sat on a grassy slope near Linda, and we smiled at each other. "I'm very proud of you," she whispered to me. We exchanged a kiss, and I rested my head on her shoulder. I closed my eyes briefly, and my head started to feel heavy. I was spent, but I was happy. Though we didn't say a word about it, Linda would tell me later that she knew right then that this would not be the year that I give up coaching cross country.

The Plant Boys help the Panther Girls celebrate their
2011 State Championship.
(Photo courtesy of Kerri Mersereau)

Chapter Twelve

RUNNING AND HAPPINESS

December 2011

The formal ending to the cross country season is our end-of-the year awards banquet for the runners and their families. I think it's important to get together and reflect on what our boys have accomplished and to celebrate one last time whatever achievements we may have earned during the past season. This year's team had much to celebrate.

We gathered in the school cafeteria, and each boy was called by name to come forward and receive a t-shirt with "2011 County, District and Region Champions" printed on the back. The top 15 boys earned varsity letters, and I presented the six varsity seniors with a framed team photo of them on the winner's podium holding the county championship trophy. I had all of the trophies we earned during the season displayed on a table that was behind me as I spoke.

"Our boys got far more out of this season than the awards you see displayed here," I declared as I reverted to my evangelical preacher mode. "Your sons got something greater that will serve them the rest of their lives. They learned how to accomplish all of the grand and challenging goals they may ever set for themselves. They learned that to accomplish something truly great and worthwhile, you have to dream it, plan it and then do it."

"Dream It, Plan It, Do It" was printed at the bottom of every email and every handout that I sent to our runners and parents for the past six months. Now was my chance to explain what that was all about.

"You have to have a dream, and you should never be afraid to dream of becoming the very best at whatever really matters to you," I said. "If you are too afraid to dream it, then you're guaranteed to fail."

"Dreaming, however, is only the beginning," I continued. "If you are serious about something that you really want, you have to be willing to sit down, make a realistic assessment of what must be done to make it happen, and set a plan for achieving your goal."

"Finally," I said, "comes the real test. You've got to DO IT. You've got to do it on Monday. You've got to do it on Tuesday, Wednesday, Thursday, Friday and even on the weekends. You've got to do it when it's hot, and you've got to do it when it's cold. You've got to do it when it's fun, and you've got to do it when it's dull and boring and even painful. You've just got to DO IT!"

"This is what your boys really got this season—the secret to success. They learned the secret to getting a medical or law degree, to being a great husband or father, to becoming everything and anything that will help them realize their own unique potential in life. If there was one thing I would add to our season mantra of 'Dream It, Plan It, Do It," I told them, "it would be one last word—'*together.*' None of us can accomplish anything truly worthwhile all on our own. We learned to work with each other and for each other. Every one of our boys accomplished more as part of this team than he ever could have done on his own. That's how it always will be. We need each other to truly succeed, and we will always be better *together.*"

Most people hate public speaking. I live for it. Nothing else gives me the same sense of efficacy or purpose. It's something that's always come naturally to me. I suppose it's one reason I thought seriously about the ministry and what I love most about being a teacher. Sometimes, however, I catch myself wondering how I have the audacity to think that I have any great truths to share or why others should care about what I think is the "secret to success." Am I qualified to preach the principles of effective living just because I have won a few teacher awards and some state championships?

It would only be fair to ask what reason I have to think that I am such a success. I'm not a doctor or a lawyer. I've never been a professional athlete or anybody famous. Who am I to tell them the secret of success? All I can say in response is there is honestly no one else's job, no one else's home, nor anyone else's life that I would rather have than my own. I've got everything I really want, and I'm happy with what I have. If being happy is not real success, then what's the point of working so hard to succeed?

The evening always ends with the seniors taking turns offering their final farewells and reflections. Several of the boys and their parents literally line up and wait to personally offer me their thanks for giving my time and energy to facilitate the boys' successful journeys into manhood. The underclassmen always leave filled with hope and enthusiasm for the future of the team. Regardless of our finish at the state meet, I always leave the end-of-the-year cross country banquet believing that our year-round striving together to win a state championship is most certainly worth the sacrifices involved.

It's not hard to convince people the hard work and long hours I put in with my boys is worth it. Most people I meet seem to understand right away the value of the work I do as a coach. This is not always the case when it comes to the risks and sacrifices I make for my own running.

"Isn't all that running bad for you? Won't you hurt your knees running all those miles?" These are the kind of questions that Greg and I are commonly asked by folks when they find out we run marathons. We both agree these questions are as stupid as they are annoying. It's most annoying when these comments come from folks who are overweight and out of shape. It's very hard not to give a sarcastic comeback like "Yeah, you're right. I was thinking about taking up smoking or binge drinking instead."

"Running makes me happy," I usually say with strained politeness. I have often tried to understand exactly what is motivating so many people to ask these same inane questions. Maybe they are trying to justify their decision not to run. They don't want to run, but maybe there's some part of them that feels they should run. I don't think anybody "should" run. It's only worth doing if you like to do it. I am not a running evangelist. I have never recommended running to anyone who didn't already have a desire to start running. Besides, there are so many other ways to be fit that aren't "bad for your knees."

Sometimes people will take the question deeper. They want to know if I actually enjoy it while I am doing it, or if I just like the way it makes me feel when I am done. That's a better question because it shows a sharper appreciation of the experience. To one degree or another, it always hurts to run. The first couple miles of every run are usually the most painful until my body has had a chance to loosen up and start producing pain-numbing endorphins. That's when I can usually begin to run comfortably. Even then, the pain never really goes away. It's not like I enter some running nirvana state. It's more like reaching a new equilibrium state.

To paraphrase the great Buddha, "Life in general is painful." But I would argue that a sedentary lifestyle is more painful than an active one. "Use it or lose it" may be cliché, but it's one of life's true paradoxes. The aches and pains of my endurance running lifestyle give me a general sense of satisfaction and pride. I love the feeling of lying around all Sunday afternoon with stiff, sore legs after a 20-mile run. Not only does it relieve much of my stress and anxiety, but it fills my mind with positive self-thoughts and optimism. I understand that "it's bad for your knees" to run as much as I often like to run. I guess I should just say that I prefer the pain and risks of running over the mental and physical risks of not running.

With the cross country season behind me, there are no good excuses left for not training the way I really should to run a successful marathon in just a few weeks. I finished December with 160 miles, including three successful long runs of 16, 18 and 20.5 miles. We spent the week of Christmas in Winston-Salem, North Carolina, where Linda's parents live, and I was able to do three quality runs in perfectly clear 50-degree weather. Two of those runs were 12-mile out-and-back runs at one of my favorite running locations, the Salem Lake Trail.

Next to the Moses Cone trails in Blowing Rock, where I run with my team every July, the Salem Lake trail is my favorite run. The soft, undulating trail meanders all the way around a beautiful 365-acre lake. It's a seven-mile packed-dirt/gravel loop with numerous scenic views. I'd been looking forward to going back to Salem Lake for weeks, but one negative image kept coming back to me. The last time I ran that trail two years ago, a Rottweiler bit me on the arm and ripped a two-inch long gash in my skin before the owner was able to get him off of me and back on his leash. It was the third time I have been bitten by a dog while out for a run.

Every time I have been bitten by someone's dog (all of which were unleashed at the time), each owner responded in exactly the same way: "But my dog doesn't bite." It's kind of like that ridiculous scene from the *The Pink Panther Strikes Again* when Inspector

Clouseau says, (read the following in a horrible French accent) "I thought you said your dog doesn't bite!" The clerk responds by clarifying, "That's not my dog." It's one of the funniest lines of the movie. In my case, however, it was always scary, bloody, painful and never a bit funny.

I mentioned to someone recently that my love of trail running has been severely hampered by my growing fear of unleashed dogs. She suggested that I buy a small can of pepper spray to carry with me on any run that might include unleashed dogs (or any other threatening animals). That's exactly what I did. Given the way things generally go in life, now that I have the pepper spray I will probably never need to use it. That would be fine with me as I would never want to cause any animal harm. All I know is that just having it in my pocket during my trail runs this past month has enabled me to feel less threatened and more relaxed.

A key part of my training plan includes doing a couple of races to get a realistic check on my progress so far and to reorient myself to the specific physical and psychological stresses of racing. I got some vicarious feedback at the end of November when Greg went to the east coast of Florida to compete in the Space Coast Marathon on the Sunday after Thanksgiving. He finished in exactly four hours in fairly warm conditions.

He ran a conservative race strategy that consisted of running with a pace group that was aiming for a 3:55 marathon. Greg said he was able to run with the group "fairly comfortably" until mile 22 when his legs started getting too stiff to hold the pace. Still, he was able to hold on to a reasonable pace and finish the race without having any major issues. Given the problems he was having with his hamstring and foot over the summer, he was just pleased to be back in the game and making progress toward his goal of 50 marathons by age 50. I was fairly reassured by his performance. Though Greg seems confident from the way I have been training that I'm going to be all right on race day, I am not as convinced. Greg has had far more successful marathon experiences than I have. Most of my marathon memories haunt me more than help me.

I chose the Brandon Half-Marathon on the first Sunday of December to be my first race experience in over three years. Greg was still recovering from his marathon so I was on my own when I made my way to the starting line just a few minutes before the 7 a.m. start. My first dilemma was deciding whether or not to keep my shirt on for the race. As I looked around at the other runners gathering at the starting line, only a couple of men were shirtless. Most runners seemed overdressed to me on the mildly chilly morning with the temperature in the mid-60s.

If this had been a normal Sunday long run with Greg, it would have definitely been a shirtless run since the temperature was likely to climb above 70 degrees by the time we were done. As much as I hate having a shirt on while running, the older I get, the more self-conscious I become about having my shirt off in public. Abdominal or pectoral "jiggling" in older men is never a pleasant sight. I force myself to wear a shirt at our team's Bayshore practices, not only because of a ridiculous county rule which requires our athletes to wear shirts at all practices, but because the girls' team is often practicing in the same area.

Minutes before the horn sounded to start the race, I removed my shirt, wrapped it up in a tight ball and wedged it between two branches of a nearby tree. It was time to focus on the race. My goal was to start out very conservatively and then run increasingly faster mile splits as the race progressed. During the first mile I tried to stay as calm and relaxed as I could. It was hard to find and hold a consistent pace. The crowd of runners included a wide variety of running styles, paces and intentions. I found myself having to zig and zag around groups of runners who, even though they started right up front, were barely moving faster than a walking pace.

At the half-mile mark I was able to find room to run on a fairly straight path as we started up the long uphill stretch of an overpass that took us over an interstate highway. As we started down the backside of the overpass I was conscious of trying to relax a bit without letting gravity pull me to a prematurely fast pace. I hit the mile mark shortly after reaching the bottom of the overpass in a time of 8:40. Given that it took about four seconds for me to actually cross the starting line after the horn sounded, this was just about where I expected to be.

About midway through the second mile I found myself shoulder-to-shoulder with someone who was running the same even pace that I was. After a couple of minutes of running silently beside each other, he finally spoke up first.

"What kind of time do you plan on running?" he asked.

"I want to hold at least an 8:30-pace for 10 miles and then try to pick it up," I replied.

"Sounds just about right for me," he said. "Mind if I pace with you?"

"No problem," I replied. "Let's do this."

I found out his name was Scott and that he ran his first marathon six weeks earlier in St. Louis, Missouri.

"Everything was going great until about mile 20," he said.

"I know the feeling," I assured him.

We cruised through the next three miles averaging a nice, even pace just over 8:25. The course followed a route that featured mostly smoothly paved four-lane roads with virtually no traffic. We ran through a mainly industrial area surrounded by large, new housing developments, many of which seemed to be only partially inhabited.

As we started mile five, we made a right turn that ended up being a nearly two-mile long out-and-back portion of the course that would eventually put us right back where we entered. There was a water and Gatorade stop at this intersection which was serving the runners as they entered and exited. I took a cup of water and a cup of Gatorade and slowed to a walk as I poured one cup into the other and then drank the mix before resuming my running pace.

Scott had moved on ahead, and I slowly made my way back up to him. Once I caught him, I realized that we were now moving slightly faster than before we entered this out-and-back section. When we got to the 6-mile mark, I pointed out to Scott that our pace had dropped to 8:16. He confessed he was motivated by seeing that some runners with whom he often trains were well ahead of us.

"Still over half the race left to go," I reminded him. "They'll come back to you soon enough." Scott seemed to be at least 20 years younger than I am and relatively new to racing. I started to sense that he lacked the experience to patiently hold back the way we had planned. Shortly after we exited the out-and-back section, he began to accelerate even more. He clearly did not want to wait for his training mates to "come back." He was off to go get them. I missed seeing the seven-mile mark so I didn't know exactly what pace I was running, but I suspected that I was also speeding up even though Scott had pulled away. Sure enough, when I reached mile eight, I had run the two previous miles in 16:24 (8:12 per mile).

The race course eventually reached another U-turn and started leading us back toward the start/finish area. When I got to mile nine, my watch indicated that I had just run a 7:58 mile. That was it. I knew then that I wouldn't be waiting until mile 10 to make my move, it was already on. When I did hit mile 10, my pace was down to 7:56, and I could see Scott about 40 meters ahead of me. The best part was that I still felt under control, and I could sense that I had more gears left. I consciously picked up my pace and started to close the gap with Scott.

I ran the next mile in 7:42. Just beyond the 11-mile marker was the final water stop. I moved over to my left to avoid the traffic. I didn't need any water, and I didn't want anything to disrupt my steady rhythm. I was feeling strong and confident. Scott started fumbling with a pack of energy gel just before he got to the water stop. His inexperience was showing once again. It was a little late for refueling.

As I passed him I picked up my pace one more time. I wasn't in the mood to chit-chat, and my competitive juices were flowing. I ran mile twelve in 7:32. The sight of the time on my watch and the realization that only one mile remained raised my spirits even higher. Then I saw the interstate overpass looming just ahead. I knew my pace was slowing as I climbed the long, steep hill, but I tried to keep my effort as even as I could. As I crested the top of the overpass I tried to relax and glide down the hill in preparation for the final half-mile waiting below.

For the first time in the entire race, I started to feel the stress of racing at the upper limit of my capacity. The crowd of runners had long since thinned out, yet I was still periodically passing runners who had gone out much faster. Though I was definitely feeling the strain of racing, my arms and legs were still moving well. I finished mile 13 in 7:40 even after slowing up the steep overpass. My legs still felt strong and fluid as I made the final turn and kicked the last straight-away to the half-marathon finish line in a time of 1:46:40 (averaging nearly 8:00 per mile).

After stopping to allow a volunteer to clip the timing chip off of my shoelaces, I looked back toward the finish line to see Scott crossing the finish about 15 seconds after I did. We shook hands and congratulated each other on a good race. I was very satisfied with my performance. Though it was not nearly as fast as I was capable of doing 10 to 20 years ago when I was focused on qualifying for the Boston Marathon, it was reassurance that I could still compete as a runner. It also gave me confidence that I might be able to accomplish my goal of having a successful marathon experience in just a few weeks.

Even though the half-marathon experience was a success, I paid the price for it during the next week of training. My legs were stiff and sore pretty much constantly for about the next 10 days. I got a massage which helped relieve some of the stiffness, especially in my calves, which have been tight throughout most of the past several weeks of training. Greg and I did manage to do 18 miles on the Sunday after the half-marathon, but it was one of the most sluggish and uncomfortable runs we've done. Even though it had been two weeks since Greg's marathon, he was still suffering the after-effects of that challenge.

The following Sunday Greg and I did two loops around the 10-mile Temple Terrace course. Because the full loop is actually a bit longer than 10 miles, we ended up with a 20.5 mile run on the fairly hilly course. At the six-mile mark, I started having issues in both of my legs. My right calf became very tight and fairly painful. I was also feeling a sharp pain in my lower left leg between my calf and my shin. I stopped and stretched for a bit, and then we resumed running at a slower pace until the pain and tightness abated enough for me to run at our usual training pace.

From that point of the run to the end, I actually felt slightly better as each mile passed. Greg, on the other hand, was clearly still not fully recovered from his marathon. By the end of the run, the temperature got high enough to make the conditions uncomfortable. When we finished, he said the effort felt "every bit as hard as the marathon." I agreed that it was a hard effort, but what I didn't express out loud was that it was actually easier than I expected it to be, especially after the issues I experienced at mile six. If this were the marathon day, however, there would still be six miles left to go, and the final six miles are often equally as stressful as the 20 that preceded them.

There are numerous books on marathon running out there that explain in detail the physiological reasons why running 26.2 is so much harder than 20. The gist of it has to do with the limited supply of glycogen in our muscle cells. Once the really good fuel (glycogen) has been depleted, our bodies start using mostly stored fat instead. Using primarily fat for fuel is less efficient and leads to a feeling of intense fatigue that marathoners describe as "the wall."

There are plenty of theories out there about how to conquer "the wall." Most of these theories fall into two categories. One group of strategies involves trying to increase the amount of stored glycogen by various means, including eating foods high in complex carbohydrates prior to the race and/or using energy gels (like the one Scott was foolishly fiddling with at mile 11 during the Brandon Half-Marathon). Both of these strategies can be helpful if used properly, but many runners grossly overestimate their effectiveness.

Nothing is a substitute for proper training and pacing. The second category of theories revolves around those two issues. The more times you push your body to run longer and longer distances, the better you become at burning fat more efficiently and coping with the presence of lactic acid, the harmful byproduct of endurance running that induces debilitating muscle fatigue. It's perfectly logical, really. The more long runs you do and the longer you run, the better you will be at running long—duh.

Easier said than done. We all have limits, and our time to train and ability to recover are limited. And the risk of injury goes up commensurate with our mileage. Greg and I have agreed that 20 to 21 miles is plenty long enough for a training run. We base this on the reality of how long it usually takes us to recover from such a long run and the time it would take to run any farther.

The second strategy for increasing glycogen stores toward the end of a marathon is proper pacing. The slower you run, the higher your rate of burning fat along with high-octane glycogen. Running easier in the beginning requires using less glycogen and, therefore, leaves some "in the tank" for those final miles. It sounds crazy to most people, but most marathoners would understand what

141

I mean when I say how incredibly hard it can be to run that slowly when the gun goes off to start a race after six months of training.

Another important benefit of the weekly long run, in addition to the physiological results described earlier, is the psychological preparation of simply learning to be patient for such a long time. The closest analogy I have for describing the psychological strain of running a marathon is long distance driving. Imagine driving for four hours without a break. Now imagine going 55 mph the whole way to conserve gas when the speed limit is 70. On top of that, you see several cars buzzing by at 80 or faster, and all you want to do is press the damn gas pedal and get there. That's about what it feels like to go out slowly enough in a marathon to run your best race.

In the car, I almost always have music playing to help me enjoy my time on the road. On my runs, however, I absolutely refuse. Growing numbers of runners are all "wired up" these days with music blasting in their ears as they run. It's become such a common sight that it doesn't bother me nearly as much as it used to. I've never even been tempted to listen to music on my runs, nor do I allow the boys on my team to wear their iPods or anything like that during our practices.

For them, I justify my no-music policy as a matter of safety and team camaraderie. Not only do I want them to hear potentially dangerous traffic, but I want them talking and relating with each other. Some coaches argue that allowing them to listen to music makes running seem easier and helps keep kids out for the team. I think that any kid who ends up quitting just because he can't listen to his iPod during practice isn't really that serious about being part of the team. I know that many of our runners wear their iPods when they run on their own and I've become fine with that.

For me, it's harder to explain why I am so strongly opposed to music while I run. I believe I like music even more than the average person. I have fairly eclectic music tastes, although I usually prefer alternative rock (new and old), R&B (mostly older Motown and funk) and blues. I'm listening to music right now (The Black Keys) as I type. So if I love music and I love running, why the strong aversion to combining them? I believe it's because I like to think of my time spent running as sacred time. Running frees me.

I recently accepted an invitation to "run with" a colleague and her training partner. We met on the Bayshore and chatted briefly while we stretched. Then, just as we prepared to take off on our run, both of them plugged their ears with earphones and cranked up their tunes. At first, I just chuckled to myself. After a while, it got a little annoying. Whenever I started to share something funny or interesting (to me anyway), my friend pulled out one of her earplugs and said, "Huh?" After a while my response was "Never mind." When we were done running, I barely felt like we had spent any time together.

The iPod craze no longer annoys me as much as it once did, but there's a whole list of things that Greg and I regularly encounter on our runs that make us cringe. Here are a few:

1. *The Sweater-Around-The-Waist*—For women it's unattractive. On men, it's simply inexcusable.
2. *The Cleavage Clip*—I have come to accept the sight of iPods, but tucking it between your breasts onto your jog bra? Puhleeze!
3. *The Tour de "Farce"*—These are the spandex-attired guys (almost always men) who insist on riding their $2,000 racing bike complete with aero-bars on the Bayshore sidewalk. Use the bike lane!
4. *The Karaoke Kooks*—It's not enough for these folks to just listen to their iPods, they have to sing along—aloud.
5. *The Phone-Fools*—Yes, we get it. You're so doggone important that you have to be on the phone chatting it up for all of us to hear.

As much as Greg and I might sometimes enjoy mocking those on my list, I know that Greg and I must be on other people's grievance lists for everything from running shirtless to our snobbish attitudes about all of the behaviors listed above. In some ways, running is like religion. Some believe in it, some don't. Those who believe in it don't always agree on the best way to do it. Some people run out of guilt or duty. The best running is done with a pure heart, freely and gladly for a single purpose—happiness.

Running unplugged on beautiful trails, like this 10-mile clay road loop in Clermont, is a source of great joy for me.
(Photo courtesy of Angel del Monte)

Chapter Thirteen

A GOOD ANIMAL

January 2012

To me, the New Year's holiday is just an extension of the Christmas season. Maybe that's because I'm a school teacher, and I've always had two full weeks off each winter that include both of those holidays. But there's also something about the start of a brand new year that seems to be at the heart of the Christmas message. It's as if we're invited to be "born again" along with the baby in the manger.

Not everybody looks at New Year's this way. The only "spirit" many people associate with this holiday comes in bottles and cans. For me, this date has become a regular time of reflection and renewal. If there's one thing I've concluded about the purpose of life, it's that each of us gets to decide what it is for ourselves. For me, I've decided that my purpose is to maximize my own unique, limited existence. We can't control the raw material we are born with, but our thoughts, our choices and our actions go a long way toward determining what becomes of the original stuff we inherited. I'm on a mission to make the best use of my stuff.

There's a common misconception that being "born again" happens overnight. Like the apostle Paul who was struck off his horse on the road to Damascus, there's this idea that once we "see the light" our work is done. It's like the fairytale endings where the main characters live happily ever after. There's a lesser-known Christian doctrine called sanctification, which stresses the lifelong pursuit of holiness. Everybody has his or her own notion of holiness, just like Christians disagree about what it means to be a Christian. If Jesus still happens to be interested in what we are up to, I would be surprised if he wasn't equally amused and appalled at the manner in which some people portray him.

Every Christian has their favorite Jesus. In the movie *Talladega Nights*, race car driver Ricky Bobby was fond of praying to the "eight pound, six ounce, newborn baby Jesus." Ricky's best friend, Cal Naughton, Jr., preferred a Jesus wearing a tuxedo t-shirt.

"I like to party, so I like my Jesus to party," Cal said with a broad NASCAR smile. Some conservative Christians prefer an uptight Jesus who seems to be obsessed with stopping gay marriage and building mega-churches.

My favorite Jesus is the friend of the freaks. The Jesus I can relate to best is the one who ignored the religious authorities by associating with prostitutes, tax collectors and the disenfranchised. He preached loving and healing, not judging and hating. My favorite Jesus would be just as happy to see two gay men sharing vows of genuine love and fidelity as he would be to see Tim Tebow pointing skyward in thanks for another improbable football victory.

Likewise, my version of what it means to pursue "holiness" is to be more like the Jesus that I like. The aforementioned apostle, Paul, summed up my vision of holiness in nine words: *love, joy, peace, patience, kindness, goodness, gentleness, faithfulness and self-control.* He called these "the fruits of the spirit." If you see oranges hanging from a tree, you can safely call it an orange tree. If you see someone exuding theses nine traits, I feel confident calling that person holy. No religion has a monopoly on these nine traits, and I know many folks with no religion at all who embody holiness better than many who call themselves believers.

Those nine words have been posted near my desk for years. As often as I can remember to do so, I take time to read each one and visualize those traits taking over me. New Year's is the one time I force myself to do a thorough nine-part "check-up." I look at the direction in which my life was going as the year ended, and I try to see the trajectory of it. Sometimes the trajectory is pointed upward, and those are the years when the holiday is nothing more than a break to get rejuvenated so I can pick up where I left off.

Some years I can see trends in my thinking and behavior that slope downward. Those are the years when I spend the holiday trying hard to see myself as honestly and objectively as possible. That's when God's call to repent echoes in my mind and soul, urging me to let go of toxic thoughts (and sometimes toxic people). Those are the years when I return to work in the New Year, not necessarily with resolutions but with revelations. Those are the times when I need to be born again . . . again.

New Year's 2012 found me nearing the finish line of this book and my preparation for the ING Miami Marathon. My self-reflection and introspection have been heightened by both of these endeavors. Writing this book has revealed some important things to me, and I'm at the point where I finally know I'm going to make it. I remember last spring being afraid to tell too many people that I was writing a book because I was not completely sure I could really do it. It's been a marathon.

My big concern now is the 2012 ING Miami Marathon at the end of this month. Greg was out of town for the first weekend of 2012, so I asked Linda to accompany me on her bike for the final 10 miles of a 16-mile run which went very well. Greg and I had agreed that we would do our final long run three weeks prior to the marathon, so the following weekend we planned on running two of the hilly Temple Terrace loops like we did in December. However, when Greg returned from his Christmas vacation, the problem on the bottom of his foot was flaring up again so he was unsure of how far he wanted to go. We decided to do our last long run on the Bayshore instead to make it easier to cut the run short if Greg's foot got worse.

I went ahead and ran three miles alone in the cool, early morning darkness on that second Saturday of 2012, just to make sure I ran enough miles to feel properly trained for the marathon. After Greg arrived we both did 18 miles together to give me a total of 21 for the day. It felt harder for me than I expected it to feel. In fact, it felt every bit as hard to me as the 20.5-miler we did on the hilly Temple Terrace course in December. I concluded that it was the cumulative effect of the amount of quality running I did over the Christmas break. My body needed more time to recover, and that's exactly what I had planned for the remainder of January.

The following week was supposed to be another race experience, a final tune-up before the marathon two weeks later. Instead, Greg and I decided to save the $40 entry fee that the local 10K race was charging and do our own tune-up. We went to Al Lopez Park, and we ran our three-mile course three consecutive times with a brief recovery between each timed run. We finished the first one in

24:18 (8:06 per mile). We picked up the pace for the second run, and we finished in 23:27 seconds (7:49 per mile).

At about half a mile into the third and final three-mile timed run, the talking ceased. The pace was close enough to our maximum effort to make conversation difficult. Instead, we each focused our effort and finished in 21:48 seconds (7:16 per mile). Given that we got to the first mile of the final three-mile run in 7:35, we actually managed to drop our pace to nearly 7:00 flat for the final two miles. It was a perfect tune-up. And there was no entry fee.

Next came the dreaded two-week wait for the marathon. It sounds much easier than it really is. There is no use trying to gain any more fitness by this time. If you do any quality running this close to the marathon, you risk not being fully recovered on race day. On the other hand, going two weeks without doing any quality running can make you feel fat and sluggish. It plays with your mind. No matter how much you tell yourself that you are still fit, you begin to imagine your hard earned fitness just slipping farther and farther away as the big day nears.

With ten days to go I started checking the extended forecast for the Miami area. It didn't look good. The forecast was calling for high temperatures in the 80s.

"You should start looking for a back-up marathon," our girls' cross country coach, Roy Harrison told me. Roy is a veteran of a few marathons himself, and he is well aware of the detrimental effects that heat can have on a marathoner's performance. If this had been 10 years ago, when I was obsessed with trying to qualify for the Boston Marathon, I'm pretty sure I would have nixed my Miami plans and tried to enter the Myrtle Beach Marathon two weeks later in the hopes of cooler temperatures.

Though I am focused on maintaining my streak of sub-4:00 marathons, the process has become more important than the final product. It's almost as if I felt I had already succeeded just by staying healthy and focused over these eight months of training. I knew I was ready to run a sub-4:00 marathon, and all I could do was hope for the opportunity to make it happen in Miami. Less than ideal conditions would make achieving my modest goal that much more meaningful. Under ideal conditions I might be tempted shoot for a faster time, and possibly end up being less satisfied just to achieve my primary goal.

"Who knows?" I thought to myself, "Maybe a cool front will get here just in time."

It almost did. In fact, a cool front did make it to the Tampa Bay area by the day of the race, but it didn't quite make it all the way down to Miami. Luckily, the rain clouds that ushered the cool front into the state did make it to Miami. Warm and humid conditions greeted us when we left our hotel for the 0.7-mile walk to the starting line (much farther than advertised on the hotel's website). But even in the 5:30 a.m. darkness, we could see the sky covered with clouds that promised to at least keep us protected from the famous Florida sunshine. We were told that the rain associated with those clouds would stay offshore. This was also a lucky break since running 26.2 miles in soaking wet shoes and socks would have presented its own set of undesirable circumstances.

Overall the conditions were not good, but not as bad as they could have been. Greg and I wore t-shirts to the starting line, mainly to avoid walking through the hotel lobby and riding the hotel elevator with no shirts on. When I took my shirt off right after the national anthem, I was hoping to feel some cool air on my skin. No chance. The air was warm and sticky, and it didn't help that we were standing in a crowded corral of runners that had grown much thicker since Greg and I entered 20 minutes before.

The downtown Miami atmosphere was electric. Lively music played and motivating videos were cast onto tall buildings. The streets were lined with throngs of excited participants and spectators, many of whom wore the kind of colorful clothing you would expect to see in downtown Miami. I heard the announcer proudly proclaim that there were 25,000 participants representing all 50 states (race results showed 4,000 marathon and 16,000 half-marathon finishers). Greg and I stayed calm and mostly quiet during the wait for the race to start. The stimulating environment reminded me of one of my earliest marathon experiences when I participated in the inaugural running of the Disney Marathon in Orlando.

It was my first real attempt to qualify for Boston, and I was very fit. Back then I was happy to try to soak up all of the energy from the early morning laser show set to motivational music that followed us through the streets of the Epcot Center in the first miles of the marathon. By the time the sun came up and the music and lights vanished behind us, I had run the first few miles so fast that I had all but guaranteed a slow, painful finish. Like many of my early attempts to run the required time to qualify for Boston, I was close. But my inability to control my early pace got the best of me.

I was careful to control my breathing and my thoughts as I waited with Greg to be released from the crowded mob of anxious runners. After the wheelchair competitors were released 10 minutes before our race start, the crowd of runners was invited to move slowly forward to take our positions for the race. Once we came to a stop, I extended my hand to Greg and wished him luck. I also thanked him for all of his help to prepare for this moment.

"You're ready, man. This is the final chapter of your book," he replied confidently.

After that exchange with Greg, I closed my eyes and tried to gather my thoughts. I thought about my family and all of those who would be thinking of me and wishing me well during the marathon. A wave of emotion came over me. Would I let them down? Would I let myself down? It's just a road race, for goodness sakes. Why was I making it into something so epic? Nobody would be better or worse for my success or my failure. Yet, I could not shake the idea that I owed it to those who loved me to finish what I had started and successfully complete this marathon.

One thing you can't miss at any running event is the number of runners wearing shirts indicating the cause for which they are running. I saw runners wearing shirts proclaiming their intent to run for a cure for everything from cancer to autism. Generally speaking, I think it's great that so many runners find a way to turn their participation in sport into an act of charity. For myself, however, I don't feel the need to run for any of these causes.

Linda and I try to be as generous as possible, and we both contribute when our friends solicit our support for their charitable participation in runs or walks to cure this or that. We contribute at church or at work whenever collections are taken, and we each support charitable efforts that are important to us. But we are also conscious of how much of our donations actually go to the cause compared to the administrative costs involved with organizations.

Running is a selfish endeavor, and I think many runners feel better about spending so much time focused on themselves when the final result can be used to benefit others. Running for a cause is a win-win for many runners because they get the personal benefits of running while others gain from their decision to combine their participation in an event with raising money for a worthy cause. For me, running for a cause is like running with an iPod. I get it. I see why others want to do it. I just prefer to keep my running as simple as possible.

So Greg and I stood there shirtless with no logo or cause other than whatever meaning we would choose to derive from the next 26.2 miles. I certainly thought about this book as I stood there contemplating what lay ahead. I was well aware of the fact that I was about to write the final chapter.

"How will this book end?" I wondered to myself. Earlier in the month I was joking with Greg that it would be an interesting twist if I died during the race. We decided he could finish the writing and probably end up with a best-seller. I mean, really, characters often die in books, but how often does the *author* die during a book? Surely that would make the book a lot more interesting.

In fact, I recently just finished reading the book, *14 Minutes*, by the legendary American distance runner Alberto Salazar, in which he does just that. At age 48, he collapsed from a heart attack while coaching elite distance runners in Colorado. Luckily for him, he was surrounded by capable responders at the state-of-the-art Nike training facility and amazingly suffered few side effects from being "dead" for 14 minutes.

Studies show that marathon deaths actually are on the rise. Last November, two runners died during the Philadelphia Marathon, a race that Greg and I ran in 2004. A 21 year old died at the finish line and a 40 year old man died just a quarter mile from the finish. This obviously raised many questions about the dangers of marathons. Research seems to indicate, however, that the recent increase in marathon deaths is more a function of a wider population of participants. In other words, marathons used to be for serious runners only. In recent years, the marathon has become more of a race for the masses.

This is not to say that only untrained runners are at risk in a marathon or any road race. Veteran competitors can also succumb to the strain, especially if there is an undiagnosed pre-existing cardiac condition. In November of 2007, professional American distance runner Ryan Shay died just five and a half miles into the U.S. Olympic marathon trial. Doctors concluded that he suffered a massive heart attack as a result of a pre-existing enlarged heart condition.

One of the most notable running-related tragedies ever was the death of Jim Fixx, a runner and author who many credit with helping start the American running boom in the 1970s. Fixx, who was once an overweight, two-pack-a-day smoker wrote *The Complete Book of Running,* which spent 11 weeks as number one on the bestseller list. Doctors concluded that Fixx was done in by a heart attack caused by an artery which was 95 percent clogged. Needless to say, this tragedy put a damper on the emerging running boom and confirmed many people's reservations about the new long distance running fad.

Lost in this debate is the enormous net gain in health by those who participate in running marathons. Jim Fixx transformed his life for the better and possibly even extended his life by running. The majority of marathon runners will gain far more than they lose as a result of their participation. Still, deaths like these inevitably raise questions about the risks of long-distance running. They also contribute to the aura of the marathon. It may not be as obviously dangerous as skydiving or racecar driving, but the badge of honor one earns after running a marathon is due at least in part to the specter of death that hovers over every long distance race.

The horn finally sounded to release the thousands of runners who had been anxiously waiting in the early morning darkness. We poured onto the streets of downtown Miami. The crowds of onlookers cheered us as we started the slow shuffle towards the starting line. I waited to start my watch until I crossed the mat that would read the timing chip in my race bib which was pinned to my shorts. I couldn't see a clock, but I calculated later that it took us somewhere between one and a half to two minutes to reach the start line. Shortly after crossing the mat, the pace began to pick up. Greg and I had to weave in and out to avoid running into other runners, and it took us nearly the entire first mile to get into a comfortable side-by-side stride.

Like the Brandon Half-Marathon, there was an overpass early in the first mile. It was difficult to see the time on my watch when we passed the first mile split, but it was just under nine minutes. Of course, that was no guarantee that we were actually running that pace. In fact, I was pretty confident we were already running faster than that to make up for the time lost weaving through traffic early on. At least I was hoping we were already running faster because my body certainly felt like I was running as fast as I dared so early into the race.

Most of mile two and all of mile three were run across Miami's MacArthur Causeway as we headed toward Miami Beach. On our right we could see the Port of Miami, where several cruise liners were docked in between treks to exotic locales. I thought about my daughter Melody, who was probably somewhere near Australia or New Zealand on a similar ship where she performs as a dancer. The week before the marathon a card arrived in the mail from my daughter. Just as I was excitedly preparing to rip into it and read the words my daughter sent, I saw a note on the back flap of the envelope which read, "To be opened on the morning of January 29th."

I almost held out that long. I opened up the envelope before I went to bed the night before the race because I was afraid I would forget about it in the stress of the race morning. I thought about her words of encouragement as we ran past the cruise liners. I felt another wave of emotion as I thought about how much I miss my daughter, who's been on the other side of the world for seven months.

My thoughts then shifted to my son Andrew, a first lieutenant and graduate of West Point. Last year at this time he was living on an Iraqi Army base in Fallujah, where he was stationed for a year. Normally, you assume it's the parents who inspire the kids. In my case, I find all the inspiration I need whenever I think of my daughter's courage to follow her dreams and my son's incredible sense of duty and honor.

As my nostalgic thoughts drifted around the world, I was also trying to stay conscious of sticking close to Greg. I was depending on him to maintain the proper pace. My dreamlike state was slowly interrupted by the growing sense that the pace felt harder than I thought it should this early into the race. Maybe I should start paying more attention to what's going on in the physical world. Our second mile time was 8:32, which was faster than we intended.

Worse yet, our pace felt even faster than that. I could tell that I was using too much energy too soon. My breathing was already accelerating, and my skin was already coated with a slimy sweat even though the skies were still mostly dark. Yikes. By the time we hit mile three at the end of MacArthur Causeway, our split time was an alarming 8:08. The realization that we were now on a suicidal pace snapped me right out of my nostalgic fog.

"We've got to slow it down!" I said emphatically. Greg was in total agreement, and we both made a conscious effort to get the pace under control.

Mile four took us to Ocean Drive on the world famous Miami Beach, and we hit that split in a more reasonable 8:40. The sun had made its way up by this time, but it was mercifully hidden by the cloudy skies. The next three miles took us past the numerous beach shops and cafes along the Ocean Drive route, and Greg and I hit all three of those splits right about 8:30. Just as I expected, we were having trouble trying to maintain a slow enough pace. To make it even harder to hold back, the Ocean Drive portion of the course was lined with spectators cheering and making noise.

As we started to make our way westward to leave Miami Beach, we once again focused our efforts on slowing to a more strategic pace. Mile eight took us to the Venetian Causeway, which would lead us back to Downtown Miami. We averaged a prudent 8:45 for the three mile trek back onto the mainland. This portion of the course was mostly free of spectators, and it also featured a few small overpasses, which helped slow the pace a bit.

At mile 11 we made the left turn that would take us due south toward the half-marathon finish area very close to where we started. The closer we got to this center of the marathon course, the more difficult it became to maintain the conservative pace. As we neared downtown, the crowds got thicker and louder, and the atmosphere became more and more like a carnival.

For the first time in the race, I started to feel like I was the one pushing the pace. Two or three times during miles 12 and 13 I found myself a few meters in front of Greg. Each time I slowed my pace to match his. After mile 13, the next time I sensed myself pulling ahead of Greg I just continued to relax and run a comfortable pace. It just felt more natural to run my own pace than continuing to try to adjust to Greg's. I also thought Greg was starting to struggle a bit at the halfway point. I knew it was a risk, but there was a sense of freedom that came with going on my own for a while.

As I made my way south, away from downtown toward the exclusive Coconut Grove neighborhood, I was careful to hold a steady pace. I checked my watch each mile to make sure I was not going too fast. Even though I was hitting pretty even splits between about 8:40 to 8:45, I could sense that I was pulling farther and farther ahead of Greg. Was he having a bad day? Am I crazy to still be holding this pace? I only need to average 9:00 per mile to run four hours. Until mile 16 I didn't really feel any distress that would indicate I was getting myself into any big trouble.

As I grinded through mile 17, it became obvious to me that I would have to slow down if I wanted to avoid blowing up. It also became obvious to me that I would not be able to finish without a bathroom stop. I could have held it a bit longer, but when I saw convenient porta-potties near the 17-mile marker, I decided to use this as an opportunity to take a short break and start again with a slower pace. Unfortunately, I didn't get the immediate "success" I was looking for when I took the seat.

The delayed response started a minor panic moment. How long can I afford to sit here and wait this out? To make it worse, I also started to realize that the temperature inside the porta-potty was extremely hot, and I was sweating profusely. There was a puddle of my own sweat growing around my feet. Once I successfully evacuated, I had no idea how long I had been in the porta-potty, but I was very relieved to finally get out. I grabbed a cup of water and another cup of Gatorade at the nearby table and I quickly walked and drank as I reoriented myself to the race.

When I decided to make this stop, I figured that Greg would probably run by while I was "occupied," and I assumed I would be unsure of where he was for the remainder of the race. I had only a faint hope that I would find him after I emerged. Sure enough, though, as soon as I resumed running and fixed my eyes on the runners in front of me, there was Greg's red head about 40 meters ahead of me.

It didn't take much acceleration to catch him, and I quickly realized that he was struggling to hold his pace. This explained why he had not gotten too far ahead of me during my break as I expected.

My split time for mile 18 (including the potty stop) was 10:22, which suggested that my potty break took a little over a minute and a half. Greg's pace felt slow, but it was a welcome break from the distress I was feeling prior to my stop. He encouraged me to run on ahead, but I was happy to be with my friend again and in no hurry to push myself back to the edge anytime soon. We were now running through the exclusive Coconut Grove neighborhood, and it reminded both of us of our training runs around Davis Islands. Our next mile split was 9:06, and we made a series of left turns that eventually pointed us northward back to downtown Miami.

A light rain began to fall and cool us down. The welcome drops briefly gave me some confidence that I would make my goal. Slowly, however, things started to unravel. First, the rain stopped after only a few minutes, causing the air to feel warmer and thicker. Then Greg began to slow down noticeably. Even though my split for mile twenty was 9:30, he was starting to fall behind me. He didn't go quietly, however. As I pulled away from him, first he cheered me onward and then he loudly recited the entire "Hail Mary" prayer—in Spanish. (I suppose because we were in Miami?) Like many Catholics, Mary is a big deal to Greg. But like most things Greg, there's always an ironic edge.

I was able to hold that 9:30 pace for one more mile (mile 21) before I felt myself crashing into the wall. My legs felt painfully heavy, and my stride was getting shorter and slower. I started to experience muscle spasms. The first one got my left calf. It was one of those spasms that catches you by surprise and contracts your whole calf into a tight, painful ball. After letting out a scream, I walked a few steps and I was eventually able to get the calf to relax. Within seconds, however, my neck went into a spasm that caused my head to snap backward. I hollered out in pain once more as I reached my hand to the back of my neck to pull my head forward and massage the contracted muscle.

Greg, meanwhile, eased right on by me without saying a word. I was glad he did not try to coax me to go along with him as he passed. I think he could tell that my body was reaching its breaking point, and it would be futile for me do anything but nurse myself back into the race. I took more water and Gatorade at the next aid station, and I took the longest walking break up to that point in the hopes that my body could recover enough to get back into an easy stride. My time for mile 22 was 10:25.

The good news was that, after the fluids and the brief walk, I got my slow, easy stride back. The bad news was that we were entering what I knew would be one of the most mentally challenging portions of the course. Shortly after mile 22, we made a right turn off of Bayshore Drive which had been aiming us directly back to the downtown finish, and we started a two mile out-and-back stretch along the Rickenbacker Causeway. This meant we ran an entire mile eastward, made a U-turn underneath an overpass, and then retraced the entire mile back to our entry point. It's very discouraging to run for two miles and come right back where you started.

I was able to see Greg only about 30 meters in front of me all the way to the turn around, and I reached mile 23 with a 9:40 split. But I could tell over the last portion of that mile that another crash into the wall was imminent. On the way back off of the causeway, Greg slowly disappeared as I was forced to gradually slow my pace. The painful spasms returned, and once again I was reduced to walking off the cramps. My mile-24 split was 10:21. At the next aid station, I took more fluids and another prolonged walking break. This time, however, every time I started to resume my running pace, my body would punish me with another spasm. I was defeated.

My thoughts went into rationalization mode. I had a legitimate excuse for failing to reach my goal. The weather was just too warm for a marathon. As if I needed any help making this argument, the 3:50 pacing group passed me shortly after I passed mile 24. These guys were way behind pace and justifiably so, I reasoned to myself. Still, it was frustrating. As I walked along and pondered these fuzzy thoughts in my head, I was embarrassed and ashamed that I couldn't dig deep enough to push myself through the next two miles and at least give myself a fighting chance.

Like the potty break at mile 17, I was too disoriented to calculate how long I had been in this pathetic, self-loathing funk. But at some point I just re-joined the race. I had no idea how slow I was moving or whether that pace would be enough to still make the four-hour goal, but at least I was in the race again. I realized that I was feeling slightly better. As my body and my mind re-engaged, I immediately started to wonder if I had just blown it with that period of self-pity. On the other hand, maybe my body was now telling my mind how to make this work.

Sometimes they say "it's all mind over matter" in cases like marathon running. Maybe that's not so. Maybe sometimes humans are too smart for their own good. Other animals seem to do just fine in the physical world without the benefit of such relatively large pre-frontal lobes for planning and goal-setting. Maybe some things have to be done implicitly and intuitively—"matter over mind," so to speak. "First, be a good animal," wrote Ralph Waldo Emerson.

My mind was spent as much or more than my body. Every time over the last few miles that I tried to focus on the mathematical questions of mileage and pace, I became more confused and discouraged. My thoughts were weak and self-defeating. It was time to turn them off. There are no more splits stored on my watch after mile twenty-four. I have no recollection of even seeing the 25-mile marker. I became an animal moving forward instinctively for survival.

The first thing I can remember that broke me out of my running trance was an overpass that would take us past the 26-mile mark and back into downtown Miami. By the time I reached the top of the overpass I was barely moving, and my entire body was screaming with fatigue from the painful climb. But the downslope gave my body some much-needed momentum. After a quick right turn and then a final left turn, I could mercifully see the finish about 200 meters ahead of me. The crowds were loud and thick on either side, and the public address announcer was urging the crowd to cheer us in.

I wasn't just shuffling anymore. I was running now, and it was pure joy! I would have never guessed just minutes ago that I could run like this again for weeks. I heard the announcer call my name as I approached the finish, and the wondrous sight of the time on the clock elicited a wave of emotion. I crossed the line with an official time of 3:59:18. A couple of tears began to roll down my sweaty face. I'm not sure why I got so emotional. Mostly I think it was joy and relief. I tried to savor the moment by walking slowly through the finish chute where the volunteers were putting medals around the finishers' necks. I wanted to soak it all in. I finally started to see clearly what moments before was all just a blur.

Greg had finished two minutes earlier and was waiting for me just past the finish. We celebrated briefly and posed for a quick picture before making our way to the chute exit. Unfortunately, the intoxication of the moment quickly passed, and my body went into a series of painful spasms that had me screaming and holding onto nearby objects (and runners) to keep from falling to the ground. Greg handed me a bottle of water, and I took two chocolate chip cookies from a volunteer. I tried to follow Greg as he navigated us out of the finishing area, but I was constantly stopping to tend to another cramp.

Our hotel was much farther from the finish area than we realized. For a while it felt as if I was back in the marathon, but I was constantly reminding myself that it was all really over and that I actually made my goal. I started thinking about how good it was going to feel to make the calls and send the texts to my friends and family who I assumed were growing anxious to know how I did. Of course, Greg and I had no shirts, and it was extremely awkward going into the hotel lobby and especially the crowded elevator.

Nevertheless, the pride and joy I felt over my success transcended my neurotic inhibitions as well as the residual physical distress. I knew that the pain and soreness were going to last a long time, but I also knew that every time my body painfully reminded me of what had just happened, that memory would elicit a deep sense of satisfaction which would make it all seem worthwhile.

Why did I run this marathon? Why do I continue to sacrifice so much time and energy coaching cross country? Heck, why did I write this book? These are the ways I have chosen to help bring greater meaning and joy into my life. We all have limited space and time to make our journeys. Each of us must choose carefully what to take and what to leave behind. Maybe this is why I like to keep my running so simple. It just feels good to leave my door, with nothing but a pair of shorts and shoes, and go for a run.

Running makes my journey happier, and it makes me a better traveler.

The Red Monkey and I celebrate at the end of another challenging journey.

Epilogue
RUN, RINSE, REPEAT

The process of writing this book has been one of the single most worthwhile endeavors I have ever undertaken. I started the book on April 29, 2011. As I type this page, today is July 4, 2012. The majority of the first four chapters was written during my spring break of 2011 while I was still delirious from my "falling in love again" experience, and the ideas came faster than I could type. I often lost total track of time and space during that period. Psychologists call that kind of work "flow," and they claim it's one of the key components to a happy life.

I wrote most of the other chapters as soon as I could after each given month was over. I preferred to get fully involved for several hours at a time rather than spreading out the writing bit by bit over an entire month. The hardest part was finding those blocks of time each month. Once I hunkered down and starting typing, I always reverted back a sense of excitement and enthusiasm for the project. As each chapter was completed, it was sent to an online folder where my incredible daughter-in-law Caitlyn would edit it for me. When the school-year ended, I finally had the block of time I needed to go back through all those edited chapters to revise and re-organize them into a complete manuscript.

It never felt like work at all. Like running, it was hard, but the act of doing it made me feel good. Also like running, the end result has made me happier, healthier and smarter. It's given me something to be proud of—in this case, a legacy. My friend and mentor Dennis Jones asked me to consider reflecting on what I've learned from my hall of fame coaching career, and I gave my very best effort to do just that. I tried to be as honest as I could without causing anyone unnecessary harm, and I tried to pass on something valuable of myself for my family, my friends, and anyone who cares about reaching their fullest potential as a runner or as anything else they may want to be.

As I reflect back on this past year, the question that comes to my mind is, "Did I succeed?" I could say that writing this book was a success simply because I stuck with it and finished it. But what if no one reads this book? Worse yet, what if people do read this book and don't like it? I could say the marathon was a success because I kept my streak of sub 4:00 marathons going. But it was also the slowest marathon time of my running career, and I was nearly 1,000 places behind the winner. Finally, I could say my team was successful (as I did at the banquet) because we won the County, District and Region Championships, but we were third in the biggest race of the season.

The success question is much like the meaning of life question—each of us gets to decide for ourselves what it is. Success is different than winning. Winning is more objective. My team won the Region Meet, but not the State Meet. That's a fact. I did not win the ING Miami Marathon, and this book will not likely win me any prizes. And please, don't even try to tell me that "we're all winners." That's just not true. Winning and success aren't the same thing. Every race has only one overall winner. We can all be successful, but we can't all be winners.

Success is more like happiness than winning. Unlike winning, happiness is something we must decide for ourselves. Psychologists use the term "subjective well-being" when they try to measure happiness. The common research methodology amounts to simply asking people to rate their own happiness. Winning usually makes us happy, and it can help define success for us. Though striving alone does not make us winners, it's certainly an essential component of both happiness and success. Winning is great, but striving to win is essential to a happy and successful life. We may want to win, but we need to strive, to dream and even to fail in order to give our victories real meaning and value.

When I was a kid, I remember reading the following instructions on the back of a bottle of shampoo: "Lather, rinse, repeat." I assumed this meant I was being told to shampoo twice in a row. Even at a young age, I realized that either this shampoo was not very good, since it took two tries to clean my hair, or they were just trying to get me to use up the shampoo faster so I would need to buy another bottle. I came up with my own meaning for those bizarre directions. I concluded that even though I might lather and rinse each day, my hair was going to get dirty again, and I would eventually have to repeat.

It's like that with success and happiness. Neither is ever achieved once and for all. We strive to reach a desired goal, and, whether we achieve it or not, life doesn't end there. Either we rejoice or we weep, and then we must move on. The most disappointing season during my time at Jesuit was 1999. It was the year after winning our first state championship, and we finished ninth at the State Meet after being ranked in the top-five all season. We had no realistic chance of winning the meet and repeating as champions, but being unable to defend the title was not what made the season so unsuccessful. We were easily defeated by several teams that we had beaten handily during the course of the season. The previous year's success was of no use to us.

The following year, however, was the improbable 2000 State Championship, which I described earlier in this book. In that case, the previous year's failure did not keep us from winning—we had "rinsed" it out. Whether we fail or succeed, all we can do is reflect back, learn from our experience and set out to try again. Every season starts fresh, and nothing is ever guaranteed. State champions must begin all over again next season just like everybody else.

Sometimes it's the pain of losing that fuels a greater desire for success the following season and even heightens the joy of future achievements. Happiness and heartache are ironically inextricable from each other. It's not possible or even desirable to strive for a life without pain and sorrow. Without those two necessary evils, there would be no way to really know the true joy of success. The longer my team goes on striving to win a state title, the more ecstatic we will be when that dream comes true.

So here I am in the middle of summer getting another group of boys ready to chase the dream, but I didn't jump right back in without some serious second thoughts. This spring I once again entertained the idea of retiring from coaching to begin some new chapter of my life. I've never been content to repeat the same experiences over and over without looking for the next challenge and pushing myself to grow. I also wonder how much longer I will have the energy and stamina for this kind of work. Teaching and coaching at a large, public high school is demanding (if you're doing it right, anyway). There is no shortage of hassles as part of a large bureaucracy.

Because of all this, I seriously considered moving on after last season, but I'm not ready to give it up just yet. Writing this book may have been the thing that has helped me more than anything else to stay committed to coaching into next year and continue the quest to bring a boys cross country state championship to Plant High School. Not because I want to take care of any unfinished business, but rather because these reflections helped me appreciate more than ever what this sport has done for me and for so many athletes whom I have coached through the years.

My final thought about this project is that I hope this book might someday help someone else the way it has helped me. Maybe it could inspire another coach not to quit. Perhaps some of the training and coaching lessons I shared might help a runner or a team reach their goal. Or maybe somebody might just enjoy their next run a little bit more. That would be pretty cool.

The family of my dreams—we did it TOGETHER.
Left to right: Me, Linda, Melody, Caitlyn and Andrew

ACKNOWLEDGMENTS

As I told our runners and parents at the end-of-the-season dinner, there's one last word essential to any great success—together. This book, this cross country season and this marathon could not have been accomplished without my loving family, good friends and supportive community. My greatest dream in life was to create my own family that was happy, healthy and loving. If I did nothing else in my life, that would be more than enough. I have them to thank for making that dream come true.

I owe the greatest debt of gratitude to my very loving and lovely wife Linda. I often joke with people that, "You wouldn't want to know me if it weren't for Linda." That's only a slight exaggeration. Linda truly makes me want to be a better man. Her careful reading of my first manuscripts not only improved the writing but saved me great embarrassment as she was able to help me see how some of my words might be misinterpreted or come across as hurtful. She didn't just read and edit these pages. She showed the genuine nature of her love by really thinking through this book with me.

My beautiful daughter Melody read most of my first drafts and was a valuable sounding board as only she can be. Never ask for Melody's opinion unless you can handle the truth. My awesome son Andrew has always been a great source of support and inspiration. He is our hero. His incredible wife Caitlyn is hereby declared the world's greatest daughter-in-law. She generously shared her natural brains and Notre Dame training to edit this book as well as her artistic talents to produce several of the images including the front and back cover photos.

I am so grateful to my friend and mentor Dennis Jones for his inspiration and guidance. I doubt I could have committed to writing a book without his encouragement. My good friend and running partner Greg Maurin also gave me plenty of encouragement in his uniquely entertaining way. We've run hundreds of miles together since I started this book and probably thousands since the fall of 1998. That's a lot of mocking.

As I wrote this book, I realized the profound effect of great coaches and teachers in my life, especially "Wild Bill" Minahan and his lovely wife Martha. I must also thank the numerous parents throughout the years who have trusted their sons to my supervision. Many of them have continued to be generous friends over the years and have made Linda's and my life so much richer. Finally, thank you to all of the young men who ran for me. I hope you always remember those days fondly. Mostly, I hope that the lessons we learned in our striving together will make your lives happier and more successful.